Programmable Networks with C++

Network Automation for SDN, Intrusion Detection, Cloud, and AI Infrastructure with C++23

Anais Sutherland

Published by: GitforGits

www.gitforgits.com

Printed in India

First Printing: August 2026

ISBN: 978-81-688699-3-6

Cover Design by: Kitten Publishing

Prologue

There was one really bad failure I caused once that took eleven seconds to create and nineteen hours to explain. I thought I'd only set up one interface, but it turned out to be four hundred. It went through the fabric super-fast, faster than I could even get to the terminal. Basically, there was nothing wrong with the command. It was just one of those things where everything about the way I had reached for it was. It was a real eye-opener, showing me the difference between a script and a tool. A script does what you typed. A tool knows what you meant, shows you the consequences first, refuses the parts that can't be true, and remembers how to walk backwards. We've all written the first kind. The truth is, not many of us were ever shown how to build the second one.

At some point, I think our industry decided that network automation was for interpreted languages and that C++ was for the data plane. For a while, that division made sense. It all went a bit weird the moment a machine-learning job started relying on a lossless fabric, a cluster scheduler, a cloud load balancer, a token gateway and a telemetry pipeline all working at the same time. I mean, ask a language to hold that much state, poll six hundred endpoints, parse a schema, and never leak a buffer over a fourteen-hour run, and the options are pretty much limited. As a result, we're going back to C++, but not the version many of us were taught. It's a result type that just can't be ignored. It's a span that borrows a packet without copying it. A coroutine that waits for a slow switch without using a thread. It's a range pipeline that turns four passes into one expression. These are not features to admire from afar. They're just everyday tools for everyday work, and they arrived right when our networks got complicated enough to need them.

All of this is explained in the program. We call it NETOPS, and it starts in the first chapter with a few structs and a parser. So, by the time you get to the last chapter, you'll be familiar with the switches over NETCONF, server provisioning, building overlays, traffic inspection, cloud network provisioning, Kubernetes resource application, RDMA fabric validation, inference traffic routing, and reporting your findings through an interface that an assistant can query. I don't throw anything out between chapters. Whatever listing you type will stay in the tree. You'll see a pattern repeating itself. We plan before we act, we preview before we commit, we gate on evidence rather than on hope, and we write the recovery before we take the risk. That habit is way more important than any library mentioned in these chapters. And we know that libraries are always changing. So, the discipline of refusing to touch production without a way back does not.

I'll make one promise, and that's why this book looks the way it does. Basically, everything here runs on your existing laptop. There's no borrowed lab, no purchase order, and no forty-thousand-pound switch. Then you've got SoftRoCE for the fabric, Containerlab for the estate, LocalStack for the cloud, and a small model for the accelerator. If there's something you can't find, we can give you the info in a different format.

So, first things first, open a terminal. And we'll kick things off with a type that just won't go unnoticed.

--Anais Sutherland

Content

Preface

These days, networks aren't just racks of switches anymore, they're also AI clusters. These days, a single training job depends on a lossless fabric, a Kubernetes control plane, a cloud VPC, an inference gateway, and a telemetry pipeline that has to notice trouble before anybody files a ticket. Even with something as strong as Python glue, it's not going to hold up at that size. But C++23 doesn't. When you get to the end of this book, you'll have a fully-fledged automation tool at your disposal.

The book kicks off with std::expected, std::span, ranges, and coroutines applied to real device work, then builds a CMake and vcpkg project with sanitizers, tests, and a containerlab fabric. Then you can drive NETCONF, YANG, and gNMI, provision servers over SSH and Ansible, program OVSDB and VXLAN overlays, automate Suricata and Vectorscan detection, and reach AWS and Azure through one interface. The last couple of chapters show you how to use Kubernetes resources on the server side, attach pods to RDMA devices through Multus and SR-IOV, and validate PFC and ECN across a RoCEv2 fabric. Plus, there'll be token streaming for vLLM replicas, your tooling will be exposed as an MCP server, and the loop will be closed with OpenTelemetry and guarded remediation. Everything's on one Linux laptop.

In this book you will learn to:

- Plan every change so it can be undone, and see it before it runs.
- Hand back errors as values with **std::expected**, so nothing fails quietly overnight.
- Read packets without copying them, using **std::span**, and let sanitizers catch your mistakes.
- Check five hundred devices at once with coroutines, and never write a callback.
- Check a change against the device model before you send it anywhere.
- Roll out to a few devices first, and widen only when they behave.
- Let your C++ drive Ansible, Suricata, and ovs-ofctl instead of rebuilding them.
- Apply Kubernetes changes safely, then check from inside the pod that they worked.
- Send AI requests to the least busy replica, and tune the connection for tokens.
- Spot trouble with limits, moving averages, and a model that advises but never acts.

GitforGits

Prerequisites

If you're a network engineer, systems programmer, or part of an infrastructure team, then this book is for you. You don't need to have any prior experience with SDN, Kubernetes, or machine learning for this book. Just some basics of coding around C++ and fundamentals of networking is sufficient.

Codes Usage

Are you in need of some helpful code examples to assist you in your programming and documentation? Look no further! Our book offers a wealth of supplemental material, including code examples and exercises.

Not only is this book here to aid you in getting your job done, but you have our permission to use the example code in your programs and documentation. However, please note that if you are reproducing a significant portion of the code, we do require you to contact us for permission.

But don't worry, using several chunks of code from this book in your program or answering a question by citing our book and quoting example code does not require permission. But if you do choose to give credit, an attribution typically includes the title, author, publisher, and ISBN. For example, "Programmable Networks with C++ by Anais Sutherland".

If you are unsure whether your intended use of the code examples falls under fair use or the permissions outlined above, please do not hesitate to reach out to us at support@gitforgits.com.

We are happy to assist and clarify any concerns.

Acknowledgement

I owe a tremendous debt of gratitude to GitforGits, for their unflagging enthusiasm and wise counsel throughout the entire process of writing this book. Their knowledge and careful editing helped make sure the piece was useful for people of all reading levels and comprehension skills. In addition, I'd like to thank everyone involved in the publishing process for their efforts in making this book a reality. Their efforts, from copyediting to advertising, made the project what it is today.

Finally, I'd like to express my gratitude to everyone who has shown me unconditional love and encouragement throughout my life. Their support was crucial to the completion of this book. I appreciate your help with this endeavour and your continued interest in my career.

CHAPTER 1
C++23 FOR NETWORK AUTOMATION

Our work in C++ occupies a particular place among automation tools. We reach for the language when a script cannot hold the line on latency, memory, or predictability, and when the same binary must run unattended for months at a time. This opening chapter gathers the features we will lean on for the whole book, and it does so through working code rather than through abstract description. Each feature earns its place by solving a problem which appears in real fleet work.

We will also lay the first stones of **`netops`**, the single automation tool which grows across all twelve chapters. By the time we close this chapter, **`netops`** will hold a device inventory, borrow packet buffers without copying them, shape telemetry through lazy pipelines, report failures which cannot be quietly swallowed, and poll five hundred devices at once without spawning five hundred threads. Nothing here asks for special hardware, so every exercise runs on the Linux machine already in front of us.

Why C++?

Predictability over Raw Speed

We rarely come to C++ for raw throughput alone. After all, most configuration pushes wait on a device rather than on our code, so a faster language buys us very little there. What we actually want is predictability under load. A telemetry collector ingesting fifty thousand samples each second must not pause for garbage collection at the moment a fabric begins to fail, because such a pause arrives precisely when the data matters most. Our collector in C++ allocates when we say so and releases when we say so, and that control is the real purchase.

The way we handle memory matters just as much on the capture path. Once we parse frames at line rate, every copy we avoid is bandwidth handed back to the system, and **`std::span`** lets us describe a region without owning it. Beyond throughput, a long-lived daemon must not drift upward in resident memory across ninety days of uptime, since operators tend to spot a slow leak far too late. So, the language gives us the tools to be exact about lifetime. Our discipline in applying them is what separates a tool people trust from one they restart nightly.

Shape of Netops

We will now decide what **`netops`** actually is, before a single line of it exists. Our tool is one binary which loads an inventory, opens sessions to devices, collects state, evaluates rules, and reports what it found. Each chapter adds a capability to that spine rather than starting over, so the code base we finish with is the code base we began. Such continuity matters, because automation in production is never a loose pile of scripts. It is one system which grows, and which somebody must maintain long after we have moved on.

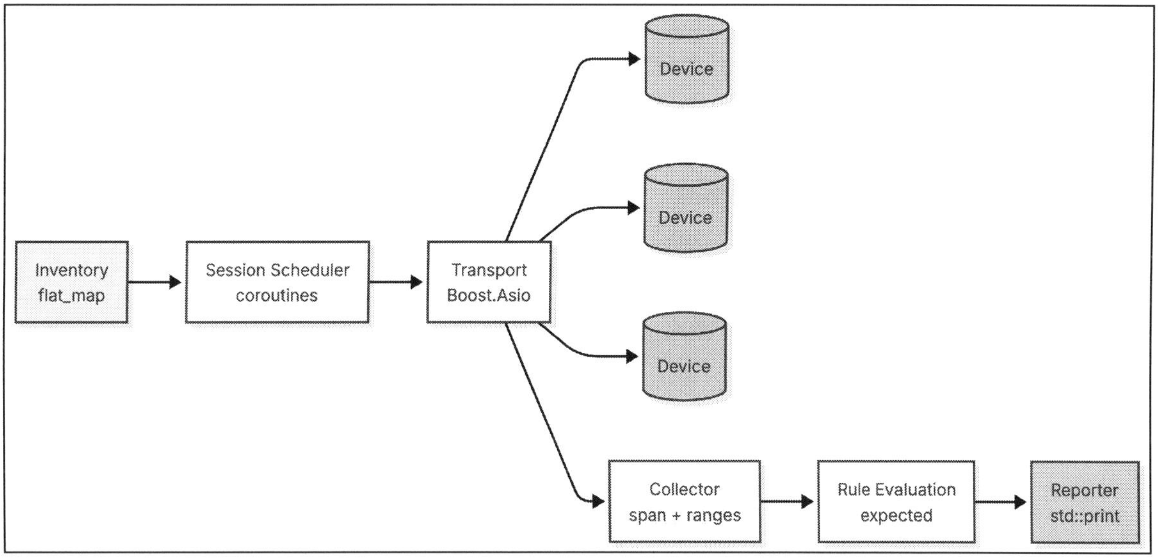

Our directory layout stays flat and obvious for the moment. A **`src/`** tree holds the components, a **`tests/`** tree holds the GoogleTest cases, and a single **`CMakeLists.txt`** ties the two together. We will not dwell on the build system here, since Chapter 2 treats CMake presets, dependency management, and the companion container image properly. For now, one translation unit and a plain **`g++`** invocation carry us far enough to feel each feature working under our hands.

Inconvenient Errors

Cost of Exceptions

An exception serves us well inside a request handler, where a failure abandons one unit of work and the caller simply retries. Our situation differs in kind. A fleet operation touching six hundred devices will see forty failures on an ordinary night, and not one of them should halt the run. Those failures are data rather than emergencies, so we want them gathered and reported rather than thrown. When an exception escapes a coroutine on a worker thread, the stack we cared about has already unwound, and the device which failed is no longer anywhere in scope.

The second argument concerns visibility, and it is the stronger one. A function declared as **`Result<Config>`** tells every call site that failure is possible, and the compiler declines to let us forget. By contrast, a function which throws looks identical to one which cannot fail, so the risk lives in documentation rather than in the signature. Our tool runs at two in the morning with nobody watching. Any path we neglected to handle becomes a silent gap in a report which somebody trusts.

Result Types across 'netops'

We will now define the two aliases which every component in **`netops`** hands back. Our **`Error`** type carries a category, a numeric code, and a human-readable detail string, because a useful report needs all three. A category lets us group failures by kind, the code preserves whatever the operating system or a library gave us, and the detail string is what an operator actually sees when the run finishes. Alongside those aliases sits a **fail**() helper which looks almost too small to bother with, yet it removes a persistent irritation. Without it, every early return spells out **std::unexpected(Error{...})** in full, and the noise steadily buries the logic. With it, a failure path reads as one short line which anybody can scan.

In the following script, we will declare the category, the error record, the **Result** alias, and a small helper which keeps failure paths short:

```
#pragma once
#include <expected>
#include <string>
#include <cstdint>
#include <utility>

namespace netops {

enum class Category : std::uint8_t {
    transport,
    protocol,
    validation,
    timeout,
    internal
};

struct Error {
    Category category;
    int code;
    std::string detail;
};

template <typename T>
using Result = std::expected<T, Error>;

inline std::unexpected<Error> fail(Category c, int code,
std::string detail) {
    return std::unexpected(Error{c, code, std::move(detail)});
}

}
```

After this, our alias goes to work in a function which parses one inventory record, since parsing is where malformed input meets our code first.

At this point, we will turn a single line into a device, or into a failure we can report:

```
Result<Device> parse_device(std::string_view line) {
    const auto comma = line.find(',');
    if (comma == std::string_view::npos) {
        return fail(Category::validation, EINVAL,
                    std::format("missing comma in '{}'", line));
    }

    Device d;
    d.name = std::string(line.substr(0, comma));
    d.address = std::string(line.substr(comma + 1));

    if (d.address.empty()) {
        return fail(Category::validation, EINVAL,
                    std::format("device '{}' has no address",
d.name));
    }
    return d;
}
```

The monadic operations are where this type stops feeling like a burden. Our loader can chain a parse, a resolve, and a connect through **`and_then()`**, and the first failure short-circuits everything after it without a single **`if`** in sight. Should all three steps succeed, the value flows through untouched. Such chaining keeps the successful path readable, which is the whole reason we tolerate an explicit result type in the first place.

To make that concrete, we will compose those three steps into one function, so the shape of the chain is visible at a glance:

```
Result<Session> open_from_line(std::string_view line) {
    return parse_device(line)
        .and_then([](const Device& d) { return resolve(d); })
        .and_then([](const Endpoint& e) { return
Session::connect(e); });
}
```

From here, what we gain is a successful path readable at a glance, and what we give up is a cascade of if statements nobody enjoyed writing. Every component we add from here hands back this same Result, so a transport failure will report itself exactly as a parse failure does now.

Borrowed Memory and Zero-Copy Views

Describing Buffers with 'std::span'

Any capture work forces a decision about ownership at every function boundary. A parser accepting **`std::vector<std::byte>`** by value copies each frame, while a parser accepting a pointer and a length invites the two to disagree with one another. The **`std::span`** type settles both problems at once, because it carries the pointer and the length together and owns neither of them. Our capture ring hands out spans into memory which it continues to own, and the parser reads through them without ever allocating.

To start with, we will add a thin view over an Ethernet frame, together with a validating factory which refuses anything too short:

```
struct EthernetView {
    std::span<const std::byte> frame;

    std::span<const std::byte> payload() const {
        return frame.subspan(14);
    }

    std::uint16_t ethertype() const {
        return static_cast<std::uint16_t>(frame[12]) << 8
             | static_cast<std::uint16_t>(frame[13]);
    }
};

Result<EthernetView> as_ethernet(std::span<const std::byte> frame)
{
    if (frame.size() < 14) {
        return fail(Category::protocol, EBADMSG,
                    "frame shorter than 14 bytes");
    }
    return EthernetView{frame};
}
```

The **`subspan()`** operation is the one which truly earns its keep here. Each protocol layer narrows the view instead of copying a payload, so a five-layer parse costs us five pointer adjustments and nothing further. Our earlier worry about wasted bandwidth on the capture path largely dissolves. One caution belongs alongside the convenience, since a span which outlives its buffer is a dangling reference wearing a friendly interface. We will therefore keep spans as parameters and locals, and never store one inside a struct which survives the capture.

Views over Device Replies

Our device replies present the same problem in different clothing. A **NETCONF** or CLI response arrives as one buffer, and the fields we care about sit at offsets inside it. Unfortunately, most code copies each field into a fresh **std::string** while parsing, which turns a single allocation into forty. We instead hold a **std::string_view** over the original buffer for every field we merely inspect, and we copy only when a value must outlive the response. Such restraint is invisible on one device and unmistakable across six hundred.

Hence, we will add a small helper which splits a reply into non-empty lines without allocating anything at all. Our helper hands back a lazily evaluated range, so the caller pays only for the lines it actually walks.

```
auto lines_of(std::string_view reply) {
    return reply
        | std::views::split('\n')
        | std::views::transform([](auto r) {
              return std::string_view(r.begin(), r.end());
          })
        | std::views::filter([](std::string_view s) { return
!s.empty(); });
}
```

In the above, our split view hands back subranges of the original buffer, the transform rewraps each one as a std::string_view, and the filter discards the empty line which a trailing newline always leaves behind. A caller walking only the first two lines therefore pays for two lines.

Should the reply itself go out of scope, every view over it becomes invalid at once, which is the bargain we accepted at the start of this section.

Shaping Telemetry with Ranges

Lazy Pipelines over Flow Records

Our telemetry arrives as a long sequence of small records, and our questions about it are almost always compositional. We want the flows above a byte threshold, with management traffic removed, ordered by volume, and limited to the top twenty. Once we write that request with loops, it becomes four passes and three intermediate vectors. A pipeline of range adaptors reduces the same request to one declarative expression which allocates only at the end. Nothing is computed until we ask for a value, so a filter which rejects most records costs us almost nothing.

In this, we will express that exact request against a span of flow records, keeping the pipeline lazy until the final materialisation:

```
struct Flow {
    std::string_view src;
```

```
    std::string_view dst;
    std::uint64_t bytes;
    std::uint16_t port;
};

std::vector<Flow> heavy_talkers(std::span<const Flow> flows,
                                std::uint64_t threshold) {
    auto selected = flows
        | std::views::filter([threshold](const Flow& f) {
              return f.bytes > threshold;
          })
        | std::views::filter([](const Flow& f) { return f.port !=
22; });

    auto out = std::ranges::to<std::vector>(selected);
    std::ranges::sort(out, std::ranges::greater{}, &Flow::bytes);
    out.resize(std::min<std::size_t>(out.size(), 20));
    return out;
}
```

Only one allocation happens in that whole function, and it happens at the std::ranges::to call. Our two filters are evaluated lazily, so a record below the threshold is rejected once and never touched again. The sort and the resize then run across a vector already reduced to the survivors, which on a busy collector is a small fraction of the input. We could express the same result with four loops and three temporary vectors, though nobody returning to it six months later would recognise the request it satisfies.

Ranges Repay Effort

That **`std::ranges::to<std::vector>()`** call is a C++23 addition worth appreciating, because the older form required a constructor call with two iterators. Our pipeline now reads top to bottom in the order the work happens. The projection argument to **`std::ranges::sort()`** deserves equal attention, since **`&Flow::bytes`** replaces a comparison lambda with a single member pointer. Both changes reduce the distance between what we meant and what we typed, which is the quiet benefit of the whole facility.

We owe ourselves some honesty about the cost as well. Our compile times grow noticeably once pipelines deepen, and a mistake inside an adaptor chain produces a diagnostic which sprawls across the screen. We also lose ground while debugging, because a lazy view holds no values a debugger can show us. So, we will reserve range pipelines for the shaping and filtering work where they genuinely clarify intent, and we will keep an ordinary loop wherever a loop reads more plainly.

Inventories, Lookups, and Readable Output

Flat Map for Read-Heavy Inventory

Our inventory has a very particular access pattern. We load it once at startup, we never insert into it again, and we then look devices up by name several million times across a long run. That pattern suits contiguous storage far better than it suits a node-based container. The **std::flat_map** container gives us a sorted vector behind a map interface, so every lookup is a binary search across cache lines which are already warm.

In the following, we try to wrap that container in an **Inventory** class which hands back a failure rather than an end iterator:

```
#include <flat_map>

class Inventory {
public:
    void add(Device d) {
        table_.insert_or_assign(d.name, std::move(d));
    }

    Result<const Device*> find(std::string_view name) const {
        const auto it = table_.find(name);
        if (it == table_.end()) {
            return fail(Category::validation, ENOENT,
                        std::format("no device named '{}'", name));
        }
        return &it->second;
    }

    std::size_t size() const { return table_.size(); }

private:
    std::flat_map<std::string, Device, std::less<>> table_;
};
```

The **std::less<>** template argument is easy to overlook and expensive to omit. With it, a **std::string_view** lookup compares directly against the stored keys, and no temporary string appears. Without it, every single lookup allocates a throwaway **std::string**, which quietly undoes the reason we chose a flat container.

Reporting with 'std::print'

The output is the part of a tool which operators actually live with, so it deserves more care than it usually receives. Both **std::print** and **std::println** give us type-safe formatting without the stream state and locale surprises of **iostream**, and they write directly rather than through a chain of manipulators. A specifier such as **{:<24}** aligns columns and turns a wall of lines into a table somebody can scan at speed. Our reports become easier to read and easier to pipe into other tooling. We can also teach the formatter how to render our own **Error** type, after which a failed result prints as neatly as a successful one.

In the following script, we will specialise the formatter and write the reporting function which uses it:

```
template <>
struct std::formatter<netops::Error> : std::formatter<std::string>
{
    auto format(const netops::Error& e, auto& ctx) const {
        return std::formatter<std::string>::format(
            std::format("[{}:{}] {}", to_string(e.category),
e.code, e.detail),
            ctx);
    }
};

void report(std::string_view device, const netops::Result<Config>&
r) {
    if (r) {
        std::println("{:<24} ok      {} bytes", device, r->size());
    } else {
        std::println("{:<24} failed  {}", device, r.error());
    }
}
```

Yet, we cannot assume **<print>** on every distribution, and a missing header at this stage would be a poor welcome. Our companion repository therefore carries a small shim which forwards to **fmt::print** when the standard header is absent, and the rest of the code never learns which one it received.

Concurrency without Callback Chains

Coroutines as Session Primitive

A fleet of five hundred devices forces an early decision about concurrency. One thread for each device reserves eight megabytes of stack apiece by default, which asks for four gigabytes of address space before any work begins. The scheduling overhead then compounds that waste, because almost every one of those threads sits idle waiting on a socket. What our workload really needs is cheap suspension rather than parallel computation, since the bottleneck is network latency and not processor time.

A coroutine meets that need directly. Each suspended coroutine costs a small heap frame holding only its live variables, so tens of thousands fit comfortably in memory. Every **`co_await`** releases the underlying thread back to the scheduler, which then drives some other device until a reply arrives. Our code meanwhile keeps the linear shape of blocking code, with no callback nesting and no state machine written by hand. We therefore stop trading readability against efficiency.

With that in place, we will trace one device poll through its suspension points, since the sequence explains the mechanism better than prose alone:

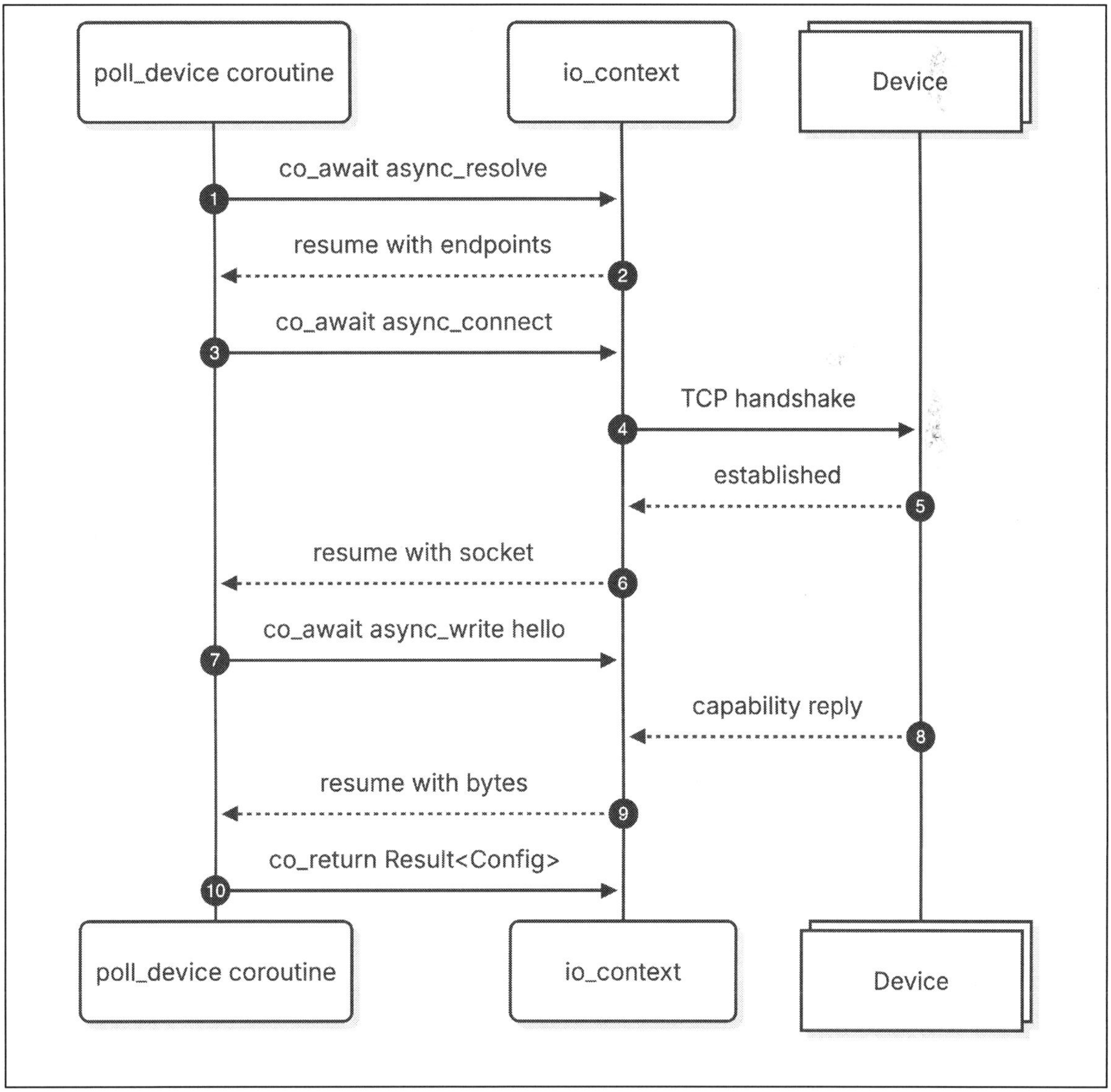

Asio as Execution Context

The standard library in C++23 gives us the coroutine machinery yet no networking to drive it, so Boost.Asio supplies the executor and the asynchronous operations. Every **`co_await`** in our session code hands control to an **`io_context`**, which resumes the coroutine once the operating system reports readiness. Our transport code therefore reads sequentially while behaving asynchronously underneath. We also gain from its maturity, since Asio has carried production traffic for two decades and its behaviour under load is thoroughly understood.

So here, we will write the first version of **`poll_device()`**. It aims to resolve the name, connects, sends a hello, and reads until the framing marker:

```
namespace asio = boost::asio;
using asio::awaitable;
using asio::use_awaitable;

awaitable<netops::Result<Config>> poll_device(const Device& d) {
    auto executor = co_await asio::this_coro::executor;
    asio::ip::tcp::resolver res(executor);
    asio::ip::tcp::socket sock(executor);

    auto [rc, endpoints] = co_await res.async_resolve(
        d.address, "830", asio::as_tuple(use_awaitable));
    if (rc) {
        co_return netops::fail(netops::Category::transport,
rc.value(),
                               std::format("resolve failed for {}",
d.address));
    }

    auto [cc, ep] = co_await asio::async_connect(
        sock, endpoints, asio::as_tuple(use_awaitable));
    if (cc) {
        co_return netops::fail(netops::Category::transport,
cc.value(),
                               std::format("connect failed for {}",
d.name));
    }

    co_await asio::async_write(sock, asio::buffer(hello_message()),
use_awaitable);

    std::string reply;
    co_await asio::async_read_until(sock,
asio::dynamic_buffer(reply),
                                    "]]>]]>", use_awaitable);
```

```
    co_return parse_capabilities(reply);
}
```

That **asio::as_tuple** wrapper is the detail which keeps our error strategy intact. By default, **use_awaitable** reports failure by throwing a **system_error** out of the coroutine, which is exactly the behaviour we rejected earlier. With **as_tuple**, the error code arrives as an ordinary value we can convert into our own **Error** record. Our transport failures then travel home in the same shape as our validation failures, and the reporting function needs no special case for either.

Cooperative Shutdown with 'std::jthread'

A daemon which ignores **SIGTERM** becomes an operational nuisance, because systemd waits, times out, and eventually kills it mid-write. Our worker threads must therefore learn to stop on request. The **std::jthread** type helps on both fronts, since it joins in its own destructor and it passes a **std::stop_token** to the thread function. Neither forgotten joins nor detached threads remain a concern for us.

In the following, we will build a small **Runner** which owns the **io_context** and a pool of joining threads wired to that stop token:

```
class Runner {
public:
    explicit Runner(std::size_t threads) {
        for (std::size_t i = 0; i < threads; ++i) {
            workers_.emplace_back([this](std::stop_token st) {
                std::stop_callback cb(st, [this] { io_.stop(); });
                io_.run();
            });
        }
    }

    void wait() { workers_.clear(); }
    asio::io_context& context() { return io_; }

private:
    asio::io_context io_;
    std::vector<std::jthread> workers_;
};
```

The **std::stop_callback** inside each worker is what connects the two worlds. Once a signal handler requests a stop, every callback fires and calls **io_.stop()**, which unwinds the pending operations and lets **run()** return. Our **wait()** method then clears the vector, and each **jthread** destructor joins its thread cleanly. What remains is a single well-defined path rather than a race we hope to survive.

Polling Five Hundred Devices

Bounding Concurrency

An unbounded approach to concurrency is a trap which looks like progress. Once we spawn five hundred coroutines at once, we open five hundred sockets in the same instant, which exhausts file descriptors, triggers connection rate limits on the devices, and produces timeouts we then misdiagnose as failures. We therefore settle on a fixed number of worker coroutines which pull from a shared index, and sockets in flight stay capped without any scheduling library. A pool of sixty-four workers across four threads suits most fleets comfortably.

At this point, we will write the worker coroutine and the entry point which spawns a bounded set of them:

```
awaitable<void> worker(std::span<const Device> devices,
                       std::atomic<std::size_t>& next,
                       std::span<netops::Result<Config>> out) {
    for (;;) {
        const std::size_t i = next.fetch_add(1,
std::memory_order_relaxed);
        if (i >= devices.size()) {
            co_return;
        }
        out[i] = co_await poll_device(devices[i]);
    }
}

int main() {
    auto inv = load_inventory("devices.csv");
    if (!inv) {
        std::println("netops: {}", inv.error());
        return 1;
    }

    const auto devices = inv->all();
    std::vector<netops::Result<Config>> results(devices.size());
    std::atomic<std::size_t> next{0};

    Runner runner(4);
    for (std::size_t i = 0; i < 64; ++i) {
        asio::co_spawn(runner.context(),
                       worker(devices, next, results),
                       asio::detached);
    }
    runner.wait();
```

```
    for (std::size_t i = 0; i < devices.size(); ++i) {
        report(devices[i].name, results[i]);
    }
}
```

In the above script, each worker writes only to its own index in **results**, so no mutex guards that vector. Our single point of contention is the atomic counter, and **fetch_add** on it costs a few nanoseconds against network waits measured in milliseconds. We therefore get correctness from the data layout rather than from locking, which is usually the cheaper place to find it.

Reading Results

After this, we can build the binary and point it at an inventory file. Accordingly, we will compile with optimisation enabled and the thread support library linked:

```
g++ -std=c++23 -O2 -pthread -o netops src/*.cpp -lboost_system
```

Once we run it against five hundred entries, the report arrives in inventory order with a summary line at the end.

```
core-sw-01                 ok      4128 bytes
core-sw-02                 ok      4131 bytes
edge-rtr-14                failed  [timeout:110] no reply within 5000
ms
edge-rtr-15                ok      3902 bytes
netops: 500 devices, 487 ok, 13 failed, elapsed 6.42 s
```

That elapsed time of six seconds across five hundred devices deserves a moment of attention. A sequential run at roughly two hundred milliseconds per device would have taken one hundred seconds, and the improvement came from suspension rather than from parallelism. Our four threads spent almost all of that time idle. We could raise the worker limit from sixty-four to one hundred and twenty-eight and shave a little more, though we would also double the load we place on the devices themselves. Such tuning is beside the point, because we do not reach for concurrency in automation to go faster. Our real aim is to wait well.

Summary

We have now assembled the small set of C++23 facilities which the rest of the book depends upon. Our **Result** alias over **std::expected** makes every failure visible in a signature and reportable rather than thrown. With spans and string views, we parse frames and replies without copying, while range pipelines express shaping work in the order we think about it. A flat map serves our read-heavy inventory well, and **std::print** turns output into something an operator can scan.

Our coroutines over Boost.Asio then gave us five hundred concurrent sessions on four threads. The **as_tuple** wrapper preserved our error strategy across the transport boundary, and **std::jthread** gave us a shutdown path we can trust. Our **netops** tool now loads an inventory, polls a fleet, and reports honestly on what it found.

In the next chapter, we will attempt to turn that translation unit into a proper project with CMake presets, managed dependencies, and a container image carrying the whole toolchain.

Chapter 2

Setting up Automation Environment

In the last chapter, we used a single translation unit to create our tool, which was enough to get a feel for each language feature. No real project stays that way. Once **netops** grows a NETCONF client, a capture path, and a rule engine, we need a build which locates dependencies, produces reproducible binaries, and fails loudly whenever somebody breaks a memory rule. This chapter builds that scaffolding once, so no later chapter has to stop and improvise.

We will now assemble a project layout, a CMake configuration driven entirely by presets, a pinned dependency manifest, sanitizer builds we genuinely run, a container image carrying the whole toolchain, and a containerlab fabric which stands in for real devices. Along the way, we settle the question of C++ modules honestly, because support across compilers remains uneven enough to matter.

Transitioning to Full Project

Source Tree

A layout decision made once saves us twelve chapters of drift. Our source tree separates the library from the executable, because every component we write must be testable without launching the tool. A **libnetops** target holds the inventory, transport, parsing, and reporting code, while a thin **netops** executable does nothing beyond parsing arguments and calling into that library. Our tests then link the library directly and never shell out to a binary. Such separation costs us one extra CMake target and repays it at every test we write afterwards.

Our directory names stay boring on purpose. The public headers live under **include/netops/**, implementation under **src/**, tests under **tests/**, and the lab definitions under **lab/**. Anybody who has worked on a CMake project will find what they expect in the place they expect it. We also keep one header for each component rather than a single umbrella header, since a change to the capture path should not force a rebuild of the reporting code.

From here, we will create that layout, which the remaining chapters fill in:

Every path in the above tree carries a reason behind it. Our **`include/netops/`** directory is the only one other targets are allowed to see, which keeps the public surface obvious and small. The

lab/ directory holds the topology and the inventory together, so a checkout carries its own test fabric rather than depending on a machine somebody configured once and forgot. Nothing here is fixed forever, and each later chapter adds files to these same four places rather than inventing a fifth.

CMakeLists

Our top-level **CMakeLists.txt** carries three responsibilities and nothing more. It declares the project and the language standard, it locates the dependencies which vcpkg has installed, and it defines the two targets. Our compiler flags belong in presets rather than here, because a hard-coded **-fsanitize=address** in the build file quietly removes our ability to choose. Anybody opening this file should grasp the shape of the whole project within thirty seconds.

In the following script, we will declare the project, find the spine dependencies, and define the library and the executable:

```
cmake_minimum_required(VERSION 3.28)
project(netops LANGUAGES CXX VERSION 0.1.0)

set(CMAKE_CXX_STANDARD 23)
set(CMAKE_CXX_STANDARD_REQUIRED ON)
set(CMAKE_CXX_EXTENSIONS OFF)
set(CMAKE_EXPORT_COMPILE_COMMANDS ON)

find_package(Boost REQUIRED COMPONENTS system)
find_package(nlohmann_json CONFIG REQUIRED)
find_package(OpenSSL REQUIRED)
find_package(gRPC CONFIG REQUIRED)
find_package(spdlog CONFIG REQUIRED)

add_library(libnetops
    src/inventory.cpp
    src/transport.cpp
    src/report.cpp
)
target_include_directories(libnetops PUBLIC include)
target_link_libraries(libnetops
    PUBLIC  Boost::system nlohmann_json::nlohmann_json
    PRIVATE OpenSSL::SSL gRPC::grpc++ spdlog::spdlog
)

add_executable(netops src/main.cpp)
target_link_libraries(netops PRIVATE libnetops)
```

```
include(CTest)
add_subdirectory(tests)
```

Here, the split between **PUBLIC** and **PRIVATE** linkage repays a moment of care. The Boost and JSON libraries appear inside our public headers, so anything linking **libnetops** needs them on its include path. By contrast, OpenSSL, gRPC, and the logger stay behind implementation files, which lets us keep them private and spare every consumer those transitive dependencies. That **CMAKE_EXPORT_COMPILE_COMMANDS** line earns its place as well, since **clang-tidy** and every serious editor read **compile_commands.json** to understand our flags.

Dependency Management with 'vcpkg'

Manifest Mode and Pinned Baseline

There is nothing that ruins reproducibility more reliably than dependency drift. A build which resolves **boost** to whatever the distribution happens to ship will behave differently on two machines, and the difference surfaces at the worst possible moment. The manifest mode in vcpkg pins every dependency to a single registry commit, so the same manifest yields the same versions in a year. Our manifest lives beside **CMakeLists.txt** and travels with the repository, which makes the toolchain part of the source rather than part of somebody's memory.

To begin with, we will proceed to declare the spine we settled on, with a baseline commit which freezes every version:

```
{
  "name": "netops",
  "version": "0.1.0",
  "builtin-baseline": "a4275b7eabc4f8d0a1f0f2f9a04e6ae0b5f5c4d8",
  "dependencies": [
    { "name": "boost-asio", "version>=": "1.86.0" },
    { "name": "boost-beast", "version>=": "1.86.0" },
    "nlohmann-json",
    "openssl",
    "grpc",
    "protobuf",
    "spdlog",
    "gtest"
  ]
}
```

That **builtin-baseline** field is the line which makes the manifest honest. It names one commit in the vcpkg registry, and every unversioned dependency resolves against that snapshot. Anybody cloning our repository eighteen months from now receives the same Boost and the same gRPC we tested against. We will bump the baseline deliberately, review what moved, and run the full suite before accepting it. An upgrade then becomes a decision rather than an accident.

Beyond 'vcpkg'

Not every library we need has a **vcpkg** port, and pretending otherwise would strand us badly later. The **libyang** and **libnetconf2** pair, the RDMA verbs headers, and the GPU health bindings all arrive from distribution packages or from source. The vectorscan sits in the Debian and Ubuntu repositories as **libvectorscan-dev**, which spares us a build. Our approach therefore splits cleanly, since vcpkg owns the portable C++ spine while the system package manager owns the platform libraries.

That split is precisely why the container image which follows matters so much. Somebody on Debian, somebody else on Fedora, and a third person on Arch would otherwise spend an evening reconciling package names before writing a single line. One image removes the variable entirely. We still document the system packages for anybody who prefers a native setup, and the image simply installs the same list on their behalf.

CMake Presets as Entry Point

Configure and Build Presets

Any build instruction written in prose rots quickly. Anybody who has followed a stale README knows the particular irritation of a flag which no longer exists. The CMake presets move those instructions into a file which the tool itself reads, so **cmake --preset debug** becomes the whole instruction and it cannot drift from reality. Our presets also carry the vcpkg toolchain path, which spares everybody a long command line they would otherwise paste from memory.

With that in place, we will define one hidden base preset and four concrete presets which inherit from it:

```
{
  "version": 6,
  "configurePresets": [
    {
      "name": "base",
      "hidden": true,
      "generator": "Ninja",
      "binaryDir": "${sourceDir}/build/${presetName}",
      "toolchainFile":
"$env{VCPKG_ROOT}/scripts/buildsystems/vcpkg.cmake"
    },
    {
      "name": "debug",
      "inherits": "base",
```

```
      "cacheVariables": { "CMAKE_BUILD_TYPE": "Debug" }
    },
    {
      "name": "release",
      "inherits": "base",
      "cacheVariables": {
        "CMAKE_BUILD_TYPE": "RelWithDebInfo",
        "CMAKE_CXX_FLAGS": "-O2 -Wall -Wextra -Wpedantic -Werror"
      }
    },
    {
      "name": "asan",
      "inherits": "debug",
      "cacheVariables": {
        "CMAKE_CXX_FLAGS": "-fsanitize=address,undefined -fno-omit-
frame-pointer -g"
      }
    },
    {
      "name": "tsan",
      "inherits": "debug",
      "cacheVariables": {
        "CMAKE_CXX_FLAGS": "-fsanitize=thread -fno-omit-frame-
pointer -g"
      }
    }
  ],
  "buildPresets": [
    { "name": "debug",   "configurePreset": "debug" },
    { "name": "release", "configurePreset": "release" },
    { "name": "asan",    "configurePreset": "asan" },
    { "name": "tsan",    "configurePreset": "tsan" }
  ]
}
```

In the above script, the hidden **`base`** preset is where our duplication goes to die. There are four concrete presets that inherit the generator, the binary directory, and the toolchain from one place, so a change to the **`vcpkg`** path touches a single line. The **`Ninja`** appears there rather than **`Make`**, because incremental builds across a growing project reward the faster generator. Our binary directories also stay separate for each preset, which lets a sanitizer build and a release build coexist without a full rebuild between them.

Sanitizer Presets

A sanitizer only helps when it runs habitually. A team which builds with AddressSanitizer once a quarter learns about a use-after-free from a customer instead. Our **asan** preset combines the address and undefined behaviour sanitizers, since the two compose cleanly and together they catch most memory faults we are likely to write. Our coroutines make that coverage more valuable than usual, because a frame which outlives its awaiting object produces a corruption which no code review reliably spots.

In the following script, we will configure the sanitizer build, compile it, and run our tool against the lab inventory:

```
cmake --preset asan
cmake --build --preset asan
./build/asan/netops --inventory lab/devices.csv
```

Should a fault exist anywhere on the capture path, the sanitizer stops the process and prints the two stacks which matter.

```
=================================================================
==4417==ERROR: AddressSanitizer: heap-use-after-free
READ of size 8 at 0x50200000eff0 thread T2
    #0 netops::EthernetView::payload()
include/netops/capture.hpp:31
    #1 netops::parse_frame() src/capture.cpp:88
    #2 netops::worker() src/main.cpp:42
freed by thread T1 here:
    #0 operator delete(void*)
    #1 netops::CaptureRing::recycle() src/capture.cpp:57
```

That report describes exactly the hazard we warned ourselves about in the previous chapter, where a span outlived the buffer behind it. The stacks show a capture ring recycling a slot on one thread while a parser still held a view into it on another. Without the sanitizer, the same fault appears as a corrupted field once a week and nobody manages to reproduce it. With the sanitizer, we receive a file and a line number in under a second. Such a difference is why the preset belongs in our habits rather than in our intentions, since a sanitizer we run beats ten static analysers we intend to install.

Modules

Named Module

The C++20 named modules offer something that header files never delivered, since a module exports an interface without having to re-parse thousands of lines in every translation unit. The build times fall, macro leakage stops, and the order of includes does not matter at all. Our curiosity is entirely justified, and so we will now write a module interface unit which exports a single function:

```
// netops_version.cppm
export module netops.version;

import std;

export namespace netops {

std::string version_string() {
    return std::format("netops {}.{}.{}", 0, 1, 0);
}

}
```

The good news is that two build steps now replace what one step did before, since the compiler must precompile the interface into a module file before any consumer can import it. That module file becomes a build artefact which our build system has to track and order correctly. The **CMake** performs the dependency scanning for us from version 3.28 onward, provided the generator cooperates. The **Ninja** generator does, while **Make** does not, so our earlier choice keeps the door open even though we will not walk through it yet.

Case for Waiting

The support situation is the whole difficulty, and honesty about it serves us far better than enthusiasm. That **import std;** line requires a standard library module which **GCC** does not yet build dependably, so anybody on a stock Debian toolchain hits a wall at the first listing. The **Clang** manages it with specific library pairings and a recent CMake, while behaviour across distributions still varies more than we would like. Our book would then owe an apology at the opening of every chapter.

Hence, every listing in this book uses headers, and that decision is deliberate rather than lazy. Our components stay small, our include graph stays shallow, and precompiled headers recover much of the compile-time benefit without any portability risk. We will revisit modules once **import std;** works on a stock toolchain across the three major distributions. Until that day arrives, a book which compiles everywhere beats a book which compiles beautifully in one place.

Companion Container Image

What Image Carries?

One image removes the entire class of problem where a listing fails for reasons unrelated to the material. Our image starts from Debian testing, installs the compilers and the system libraries, bootstraps vcpkg at our pinned baseline, and pre-builds the manifest so the first configure completes in seconds rather than in twenty minutes. The containerlab tool and the Docker client arrive as well, because our test fabric runs alongside the tooling.

Accordingly, we will write the **Dockerfile** which carries the whole toolchain:

```
FROM debian:testing-slim

RUN apt-get update && apt-get install -y --no-install-recommends \
        g++-14 clang-19 clang-tidy-19 cmake ninja-build git curl
zip pkg-config \
        libyang-dev libnetconf2-dev libssh-dev libnl-3-dev \
        libpcap-dev libtins-dev libvectorscan-dev libnetfilter-
queue-dev \
        rdma-core librdmacm-dev iproute2 iputils-ping tcpdump \
    && rm -rf /var/lib/apt/lists/*

ENV VCPKG_ROOT=/opt/vcpkg
RUN git clone --depth 1 https://github.com/microsoft/vcpkg
$VCPKG_ROOT \
    && $VCPKG_ROOT/bootstrap-vcpkg.sh -disableMetrics

WORKDIR /work
COPY vcpkg.json /work/
RUN $VCPKG_ROOT/vcpkg install --triplet x64-linux

ENV CC=gcc-14 CXX=g++-14
CMD ["/bin/bash"]
```

In the above, we copy **vcpkg.json** before the rest of the source, and that ordering is a deliberate trick. That way, Docker caches the resulting layer, so editing a source file never triggers a dependency rebuild, while editing the manifest correctly does. Our image also pins **g++-14** and **clang-19** explicitly rather than trusting whichever compiler happens to be the default. We depend on such small acts of pedantry far more than on anything clever.

Working inside Image

We will now mount our working tree into the image rather than copying it, because editing on the host and building inside the container suits most habits. That **--network host** flag matters more than it first appears, since containerlab devices become reachable at their management addresses without extra plumbing. We also add **SYS_PTRACE**, because the sanitizers and **gdb** both refuse to work properly without it.

From here, we will build the image once and open a shell inside it:

```
docker build -t netops-dev .
docker run -it --rm \
```

```
    --network host \
    --cap-add SYS_PTRACE \
    --security-opt seccomp=unconfined \
    -v "$PWD":/work \
    netops-dev
```

Now here, inside the shell, our whole build reduces to the two preset commands we already know. The presets locate vcpkg through **VCPKG_ROOT**, which the image sets for us, so no path arguments are ever needed. Anybody preferring a native setup can install the same package list and reach an identical result, and the image merely removes an evening of package archaeology.

Test Fabric with 'Containerlab'

Describing Topology

We rarely have real devices to spare, since they are expensive and usually carrying production traffic. The containerlab tool gives us a fabric described in one YAML file and started in under a minute, built from container images of genuine network operating systems. The Nokia SR Linux image carries our NETCONF and gNMI work, because it pulls freely and its OpenConfig support is honest. We deliberately avoid images which demand a vendor account, since a paywall between a chapter and its exercise makes the exercise worthless.

We will now describe a two-switch fabric with a client node running our development image:

```yaml
name: netops

topology:
  nodes:
    srl1:
      kind: nokia_srlinux
      image: ghcr.io/nokia/srlinux:24.10.1
      mgmt-ipv4: 172.20.20.11
    srl2:
      kind: nokia_srlinux
      image: ghcr.io/nokia/srlinux:24.10.1
      mgmt-ipv4: 172.20.20.12
    client:
      kind: linux
      image: netops-dev:latest
      mgmt-ipv4: 172.20.20.20

  links:
    - endpoints: ["srl1:e1-1", "srl2:e1-1"]
    - endpoints: ["client:eth1", "srl1:e1-2"]
```

These above static management addresses are worth the extra three lines. Our inventory file can then name devices by address without any discovery step, and a rebuilt lab keeps the same addresses so nothing needs editing. The **`client`** node runs our development image inside the fabric, which lets **`netops`** reach the switches across a data-plane link rather than only over the management network.

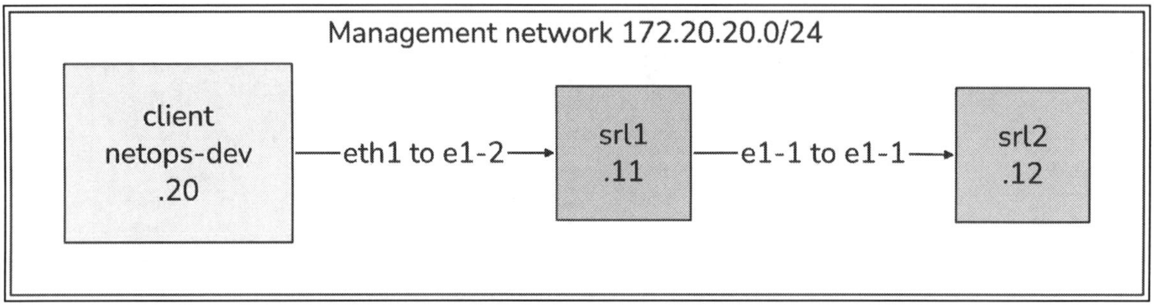

The above diagram illustrates very well the fabric before we start it.

Reaching Fabric from Netops

We can now start the fabric and then point our tool at it, which closes the loop between build tooling and work resembling the real thing. The first startup takes roughly forty seconds, after which the management addresses respond to ordinary SSH.

In the following script, we will deploy the topology, build with the debug preset, and run against the two switches:

```
sudo containerlab deploy -t lab/netops.clab.yml
cmake --preset debug
cmake --build --preset debug
./build/debug/netops --inventory lab/devices.csv
```

After this, both the switches now respond with their capability sets, and our reporting function renders them in the same columns as before.

```
srl1                      ok      2874 bytes
srl2                      ok      2874 bytes
netops: 2 devices, 2 ok, 0 failed, elapsed 0.31 s
```

At first glance, having two devices instead of five hundred might seem like a step backwards, but it's actually the opposite. Our earlier run proved the concurrency model against a file of names, while this run proves the transport against software which genuinely speaks the protocol. Both kinds of testing matter, and neither one substitutes for the other. The next chapter formalises that distinction into a strategy we can automate.

Continuous Integration for Bad Merges

Pipeline Stages

A test suite nobody runs is documentation of good intentions. Our pipeline therefore fires on every push and refuses a merge whenever anything fails, which is the only enforcement mechanism that survives a busy week. There are four stages that cover our needs, namely a release build with warnings as errors, a debug build with the unit tests, a sanitizer run, and a **`clang-tidy`** pass across the changed files.

Once this is in place, we can define that pipeline against the very same image our development shell uses:

```
name: netops
on: [push, pull_request]

jobs:
  build:
    runs-on: ubuntu-latest
    container: ghcr.io/gitforgits/netops-dev:latest
    strategy:
      matrix:
        preset: [release, debug, asan, tsan]
    steps:
      - uses: actions/checkout@v4
      - run: cmake --preset ${{ matrix.preset }}
      - run: cmake --build --preset ${{ matrix.preset }}
      - run: ctest --test-dir build/${{ matrix.preset }} --output-
on-failure
        if: matrix.preset != 'release'

  tidy:
    runs-on: ubuntu-latest
    container: ghcr.io/gitforgits/netops-dev:latest
    steps:
      - uses: actions/checkout@v4
      - run: cmake --preset debug
      - run: |
          clang-tidy-19 -p build/debug \
            $(git diff --name-only origin/main -- '*.cpp')
```

We then run this pipeline inside our own image, and that detail is what makes the result trustworthy. A green build on a runner carrying different library versions tells us very little about anybody else's machine. With the same image on both sides, a failure in the pipeline reproduces locally through one **docker run**, and the gap between the two environments closes entirely.

Refusal to Pass Through

The rules matter far less than our willingness to enforce them, so ours stay few and absolute. A compiler warning fails the build, because a warning tolerated once becomes a warning ignored forever. Any sanitizer finding fails the build as well, since memory faults inside a long-lived daemon are the expensive kind. Every new public header without a matching test fails review, as untested interfaces attract callers considerably faster than they attract tests.

One further rule concerns dependency changes. Any edit to **vcpkg.json** requires the baseline bump and the full suite inside the same commit, so nobody upgrades Boost quietly on a Friday afternoon. Our tooling now enforces what we would otherwise merely intend, and such enforcement is the whole reason for building this scaffolding before the interesting code arrives. A discipline written into a file outlasts one held only in the head.

Summary

We have now turned one translation unit into a project which will carry eleven further chapters. Our layout separates a testable library from a thin executable, our **CMakeLists.txt** declares intent while presets carry the flags, and **vcpkg.json** pins every portable dependency to a single registry commit. The system libraries which sit outside vcpkg are documented and installed by the container image, so nobody spends an evening reconciling package names across distributions.

We also settled the module question by choosing headers deliberately, and we gained sanitizer presets, a containerlab fabric of two SR Linux switches, and a pipeline running inside the same image we develop in. Our tool now builds reproducibly and speaks to software which genuinely implements the protocols. In the next chapter, we turn this scaffolding toward the discipline of writing automation which can be tested, validated, and rolled back safely.

CHAPTER 3

WRITING, TESTING, AND VALIDATING AUTOMATION SCRIPTS

Now, our system reliably builds, tests and ships, so the next question is what we are going to put inside it. One thing to watch out for is automation that changes the network state, because a script run twice can't cause any damage on the second attempt. This chapter takes that concern and turns it into design rules and then into working code. We will treat every change as a plan we can check before we apply it, and every application as something we can verify and undo.

We will now add a change-plan abstraction to **`netops`**, together with a dry-run mode which shares one code path with the real thing. After that, GoogleTest covers the pure logic, fake transports let us inject failures nobody could reproduce on demand, and integration tests run against the containerlab fabric from the previous chapter. Our final section stages a fleet change in waves and reverses it automatically whenever a health gate fails.

Idempotency as Design Constraint

What Makes Operation Repeatable?

An idempotent operation reaches the same end state whether we run it once or forty times. In practice, most automation failures we have all lived through come from operations lacking that property. A script which appends a route rather than asserting one leaves four copies behind after four retries, while a script which increments a description suffix produces names nobody can read. We cannot avoid retries in fleet work, since timeouts and transient failures arrive every single night. So, our operations must tolerate repetition by design rather than by luck.

Two habits give us that property almost for free. We describe the state we want rather than the action to perform, and we read the current state before deciding whether any action is needed at all. A device already holding the desired configuration receives nothing, which makes a second run cheap as well as safe. Such reading costs one extra round trip, and the protection it buys is worth considerably more than the milliseconds it spends.

ChangePlan over Command

We will now separate deciding from doing, because the two concerns fail in entirely different ways. A **`ChangePlan`** holds the steps we intend to take on one device, each carrying a target path, a desired value, and the value we actually observed. Nothing in the plan touches the network, so we can compute it, print it, store it, and compare it against a later plan. Our executor then receives a plan and nothing else whatsoever.

In the following script, we will declare the action kinds, the step record, and the plan which carries them:

```
#pragma once
#include <netops/error.hpp>
#include <algorithm>
#include <string>
```

```cpp
#include <vector>

namespace netops {

enum class Action { none, create, update, remove };

struct Step {
    std::string path;
    std::string desired;
    std::string observed;
    Action action = Action::none;
};

struct ChangePlan {
    std::string device;
    std::vector<Step> steps;

    bool empty() const {
        return std::ranges::none_of(steps, [](const Step& s) {
            return s.action != Action::none;
        });
    }
};

}
```

That **`empty()`** helper looks trivial and carries real weight. A plan whose every step resolves to **`Action::none`** means the device already holds the state we wanted, so our executor skips it entirely and our report says converged rather than changed. Our fleet runs then produce short reports on quiet nights and long reports whenever something has drifted. Anybody scanning that output learns what moved without reading past it.

So here, we will then compute a plan by comparing what we want against what the device reports:

```cpp
Result<ChangePlan> plan_for(const Device& d,
                            const DesiredState& want,
                            Transport& t) {
    auto observed = t.read(want.paths());
    if (!observed) {
        return std::unexpected(observed.error());
    }

    ChangePlan plan{.device = d.name};
    for (const auto& [path, value] : want.entries()) {
        const auto it = observed->find(path);
        Step s{.path = path, .desired = value};
```

```
        if (it == observed->end()) {
            s.action = Action::create;
        } else {
            s.observed = it->second;
            s.action = (s.observed == value) ? Action::none :
Action::update;
        }
        plan.steps.push_back(std::move(s));
    }
    return plan;
}
```

Accordingly, we will draw the decision our planner makes for every path:

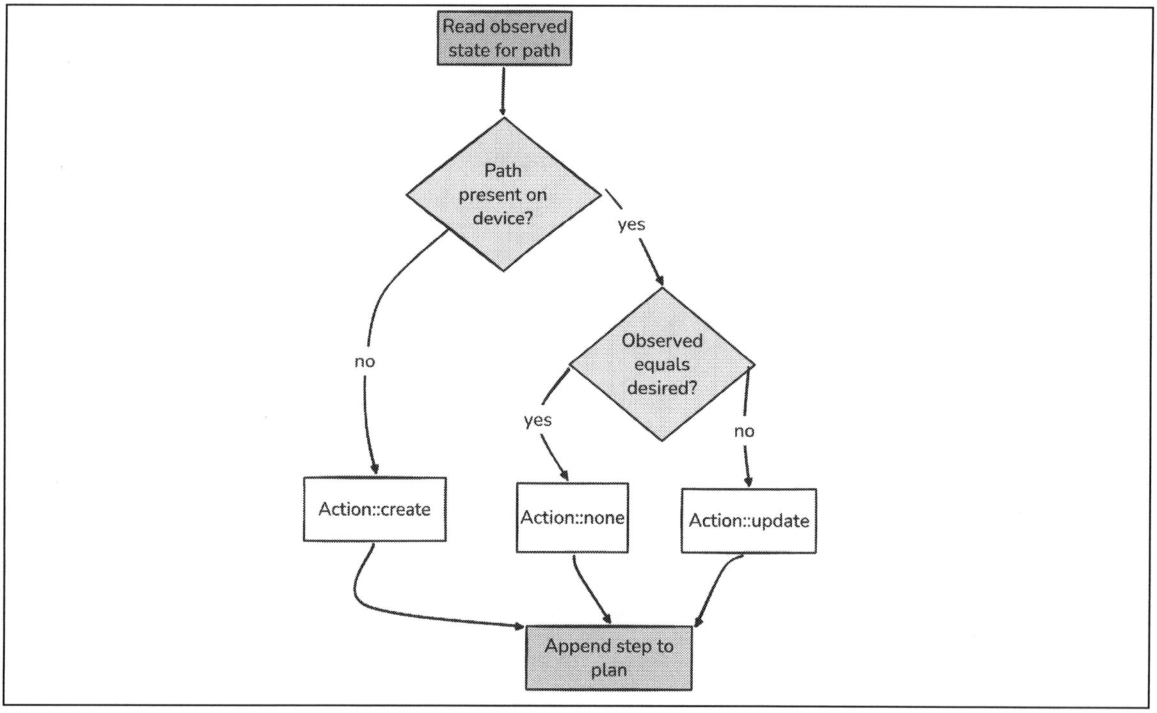

Dry Run as First-Class Mode

One Code Path and Two Behaviours

A dry-run mode bolted on as an afterthought will lie to us eventually. Two separate code paths drift apart over a few months, and the preview stops matching what an apply actually does. Our design avoids that trap by keeping one planner and swapping only the executor behind an interface. The planning code cannot tell which executor it holds, so a preview exercises every decision the real run would make. Only the final write differs between the two.

We will now define that interface with two implementations behind it. Our **RealExecutor** sends the edit and commits it, while **DryExecutor** records what it would have sent and reports success. Both satisfy the same contract, so a test can substitute either one without the planner noticing anything. Somebody reviewing a change then sees precisely the steps which would run against their fleet.

At this point, we will write the executor interface and both implementations:

```
class Executor {
public:
    virtual ~Executor() = default;
    virtual Result<void> apply(const ChangePlan& plan) = 0;
};

class DryExecutor final : public Executor {
public:
    Result<void> apply(const ChangePlan& plan) override {
        recorded_.push_back(plan);
        return {};
    }
    const std::vector<ChangePlan>& recorded() const { return
recorded_; }

private:
    std::vector<ChangePlan> recorded_;
};

class RealExecutor final : public Executor {
public:
    explicit RealExecutor(Transport& t) : t_(t) {}

    Result<void> apply(const ChangePlan& plan) override {
        if (plan.empty()) {
            return {};
        }
        return t_.edit(plan).and_then([this] { return t_.commit();
});
    }

private:
    Transport& t_;
};
```

Both implementations satisfy one contract, and the planner above them cannot tell which it holds. Our **DryExecutor** records each plan and reports success, so a preview walks every decision a real run would make and writes nothing anywhere. Our **RealExecutor** sends the edit and commits only once the edit succeeded, since a commit after a failed edit would publish a half-formed configuration. That empty-plan check at the top matters more than its two lines suggest, because a device already holding the state we wanted should cost us nothing rather than an unnecessary write.

Rendering Plan for Developer Review

Our plan means very little until somebody can read it quickly. A rendering which shows the path, the observed value, and the desired value side by side lets an operator spot a mistake within seconds. We keep the format stable and column-aligned, because stable output diffs cleanly between one run and the next. Any colour stays out of it, since our output lands in a log file far more often than on a screen.

Now we will run the tool in dry-run mode against the fabric inventory:

```
./build/debug/netops --inventory lab/devices.csv \
                     --desired lab/uplink.yaml --dry-run
```

Both switches now report what would happen, and the two reports differ in exactly the way we hoped.

```
plan for srl1
  update   /interface[name=ethernet-1/2]/admin-state    disable ->
enable
  create   /interface[name=ethernet-1/2]/description    <absent> ->
uplink-to-srl2
plan for srl2
  converged, no steps
```

In that output, two devices produce two very different reports, which is the whole purpose of the exercise. Our first switch needs an interface enabled and a description added, while the second already holds the state we wanted. An operator reviewing that output approves a change they understand rather than a command they hope is correct. We will therefore make **--dry-run** the default for any operation touching more than ten devices, and require an explicit **--apply** before anything proceeds. Such a default costs one keystroke and buys a preview which cannot lie, and that is worth more than a rollback we merely hope works.

Unit Tests with GoogleTest

Wiring Tests into Build

Our **tests/CMakeLists.txt** stayed empty in the previous chapter, and we will fill it now. The GoogleTest package arrives through vcpkg, so the manifest already carries it and no download step appears anywhere in our build. Each test file links **libnetops** directly, which is exactly why we split the library away from the executable. The **gtest_discover_tests** command then registers every case with CTest automatically, so nobody maintains a list by hand.

We will now write the test target and let discovery do the bookkeeping:

```
find_package(GTest CONFIG REQUIRED)
include(GoogleTest)

add_executable(netops_tests
    test_inventory.cpp
    test_plan.cpp
    test_transport.cpp
)
target_link_libraries(netops_tests PRIVATE libnetops
GTest::gtest_main)
gtest_discover_tests(netops_tests PROPERTIES LABELS unit)
```

That **GTest::gtest_main** target supplies the **main()** function, so our test files hold nothing beyond cases. The discovery of cases happens at build time rather than at run time, which means **ctest** knows every case name and can run a single one by pattern. A failing case then reruns in isolation through **ctest -R PlanTest.SkipsConvergedPaths**, and our feedback loop shrinks from minutes down to a second.

Testing Pure Logic First

Our planner is pure logic, since it takes a desired state and an observed state and produces a plan. Nothing inside it touches a socket, which makes it the cheapest and most valuable thing we can test. We will therefore cover the branches of the planning decision, namely a created path, an updated path, a converged path, and a failed read. Each case runs in microseconds, so the whole set stays fast enough to run on every save.

In the following script, we will assert the create branch and the converged branch:

```
#include <gtest/gtest.h>
#include <netops/plan.hpp>

using namespace netops;
```

```
TEST(PlanTest, MarksAbsentPathAsCreate) {
    FakeTransport t;
    t.set_observed({});

    DesiredState want{{"/interface[name=e1-2]/description",
"uplink"}};
    const auto plan = plan_for(Device{"srl1", "172.20.20.11"},
want, t);

    ASSERT_TRUE(plan.has_value());
    ASSERT_EQ(plan->steps.size(), 1u);
    EXPECT_EQ(plan->steps[0].action, Action::create);
    EXPECT_FALSE(plan->empty());
}

TEST(PlanTest, SkipsConvergedPaths) {
    FakeTransport t;
    t.set_observed({{"/interface[name=e1-2]/admin-state",
"enable"}});

    DesiredState want{{"/interface[name=e1-2]/admin-state",
"enable"}};
    const auto plan = plan_for(Device{"srl2", "172.20.20.12"},
want, t);

    ASSERT_TRUE(plan.has_value());
    EXPECT_EQ(plan->steps[0].action, Action::none);
    EXPECT_TRUE(plan->empty());
}
```

Once we run the unit label through CTest, the whole set completes before we can look away.

```
Test project /work/build/debug
    Start 1: PlanTest.MarksAbsentPathAsCreate
1/4 Test #1: PlanTest.MarksAbsentPathAsCreate ......   Passed
0.01 sec
    Start 2: PlanTest.SkipsConvergedPaths
2/4 Test #2: PlanTest.SkipsConvergedPaths .........   Passed   0.01
sec
100% tests passed, 0 tests failed out of 4
```

Both cases assert on the plan rather than on any device behaviour, and that distinction keeps them honest. A test needing a switch is an integration test wearing a unit test costume, and it will eventually fail for reasons unrelated to our logic. We keep the two kinds physically separate, so a broken lab never reports itself as a broken planner. That separation also buys us speed, since our whole unit suite finishes well inside a second.

Test Doubles for Transports

Faked Interface

Our planner already accepts a **`Transport&`** rather than a concrete session, and that earlier choice now repays itself. A narrow interface with three methods is easy to fake, whereas a wide one becomes a second implementation nobody maintains. We deliberately keep **`read`**, **`edit`**, and **`commit`** as the entire contract, and everything protocol-specific hides behind them. The next chapter is going to supply the **`NETCONF`** implementation of exactly this interface.

Once this is in place, we will write a fake which both supplies state and records what happened to it:

```
class FakeTransport final : public Transport {
public:
    void set_observed(std::map<std::string, std::string> state) {
        observed_ = std::move(state);
    }
    void fail_read(Error e) { read_error_ = std::move(e); }
    void fail_commit(Error e) { commit_error_ = std::move(e); }

    Result<std::map<std::string, std::string>>
    read(const std::vector<std::string>&) override {
        if (read_error_) {
            return std::unexpected(*read_error_);
        }
        return observed_;
    }

    Result<void> edit(const ChangePlan& p) override {
        applied_.push_back(p);
        return {};
    }

    Result<void> commit() override {
        if (commit_error_) {
            return std::unexpected(*commit_error_);
        }
        committed_ = true;
        return {};
    }
```

```
    bool committed() const { return committed_; }
    const std::vector<ChangePlan>& applied() const { return
applied_; }

private:
    std::map<std::string, std::string> observed_;
    std::optional<Error> read_error_;
    std::optional<Error> commit_error_;
    std::vector<ChangePlan> applied_;
    bool committed_ = false;
};
```

Our fake performs two jobs at once, since it supplies state and also records what our code did with it. That recording matters as much as the supplying, because a test asserting that nothing was committed needs some way to check. The **committed()** and **applied()** accessors give us that visibility without any mocking framework at all. Our simplicity here is deliberate, as a hand-written fake stays readable while a chain of mock expectations rarely does.

Injecting Failures on Purpose

The failures nobody can reproduce are precisely the ones which reach production. A commit rejected by a device under load, a read timing out midway through a fleet run, a transport dropping after the edit yet before the commit, all of these arrive monthly and none of them arrive on demand. Our fake reduces each one to a single line in a test, which turns an untestable path into an ordinary case. We will therefore cover the failure branches with the same rigour as the successful ones.

With that in place, we will assert that a rejected commit leaves nothing behind, and that a converged device is never touched:

```
TEST(ApplyTest, LeavesNothingCommittedWhenCommitFails) {
    FakeTransport t;
    t.set_observed({{"/interface[name=e1-2]/admin-state",
"disable"}});
    t.fail_commit(Error{Category::protocol, EPERM, "commit
rejected"});

    DesiredState want{{"/interface[name=e1-2]/admin-state",
"enable"}};
    const auto plan = plan_for(Device{"srl1", "172.20.20.11"},
want, t);
    ASSERT_TRUE(plan.has_value());

    RealExecutor exec(t);
    const auto applied = exec.apply(*plan);
```

```
    ASSERT_FALSE(applied.has_value());
    EXPECT_EQ(applied.error().category, Category::protocol);
    EXPECT_FALSE(t.committed());
}

TEST(ApplyTest, SkipsTransportEntirelyWhenConverged) {
    FakeTransport t;
    t.set_observed({{"/interface[name=e1-2]/admin-state",
"enable"}});

    DesiredState want{{"/interface[name=e1-2]/admin-state",
"enable"}};
    const auto plan = plan_for(Device{"srl2", "172.20.20.12"},
want, t);

    RealExecutor exec(t);
    EXPECT_TRUE(exec.apply(*plan).has_value());
    EXPECT_TRUE(t.applied().empty());
}
```

That second case deserves a moment, because it asserts an absence rather than a result. A converged device must receive no edit whatsoever, and only a recording fake can prove that nothing was sent. Our idempotency claim from earlier then stops being an intention and becomes a property the suite enforces. Anybody later optimising the planner will break that test rather than break a fleet.

Integration Tests against Fabric

Lab-Owned Fixtures

Our unit tests prove our logic, while integration tests prove our assumptions about devices. Both kinds matter, and the second kind fails for entirely different reasons. Our fixture therefore owns the lab lifecycle, since a test assuming a running fabric produces a baffling failure whenever the fabric is absent. A global environment deploys the topology once, and each case then runs against the same two switches.

We will now write that environment together with the entry point which installs it:

```
class FabricSuite : public ::testing::Environment {
public:
    void SetUp() override {
        ASSERT_EQ(std::system(
            "containerlab deploy -t lab/netops.clab.yml --
```

```
reconfigure"), 0);
        wait_for_port("172.20.20.11", 830,
std::chrono::seconds(90));
        wait_for_port("172.20.20.12", 830,
std::chrono::seconds(90));
    }

    void TearDown() override {
        std::system("containerlab destroy -t lab/netops.clab.yml");
    }
};

int main(int argc, char** argv) {
    ::testing::InitGoogleTest(&argc, argv);
    ::testing::AddGlobalTestEnvironment(new FabricSuite);
    return RUN_ALL_TESTS();
}
```

That **`wait_for_port`** call is the line which saves us from flaky results. The SR Linux image accepts SSH before its management server finishes loading, so a test connecting too early fails with a confusing protocol error. We poll until port 830 responds and only then proceed, which trades ninety seconds of patience for repeatable outcomes. Our integration binary also stays separate from the unit binary, so **`ctest -L unit`** never touches Docker at all.

Asserting Convergence

A tempting mistake awaits us here, since asserting on the exact reply from a device couples our suite to one firmware version. An upgrade then breaks forty tests which were never about the upgrade. We therefore assert on convergence instead, meaning we apply a plan, recompute it, and require the second plan to be empty. Such an assertion holds across firmware versions, vendors, and reply formats, because it tests the property we actually care about.

Accordingly, we will write the convergence test against the first switch:

```
TEST(FabricTest, SecondApplyIsAlwaysConverged) {
    NetconfTransport t("172.20.20.11", 830, "admin");
    const Device d{"srl1", "172.20.20.11"};
    DesiredState want{
        {"/interface[name=ethernet-1/2]/admin-state", "enable"},
        {"/interface[name=ethernet-1/2]/description", "uplink-to-
srl2"}};

    auto first = plan_for(d, want, t);
    ASSERT_TRUE(first.has_value());
```

```
    RealExecutor exec(t);
    ASSERT_TRUE(exec.apply(*first).has_value());

    auto second = plan_for(d, want, t);
    ASSERT_TRUE(second.has_value());
    EXPECT_TRUE(second->empty()) << "device did not converge after
apply";
}
```

Both fabric cases now pass, and the timings tell us where our patience goes.

```
Test project /work/build/debug
1/2 Test #1: FabricTest.SecondApplyIsAlwaysConverged ...   Passed
4.12 sec
2/2 Test #2: FabricTest.RejectsInvalidLeafValue .........   Passed
1.88 sec
100% tests passed, 0 tests failed out of 2
```

Those four seconds for the first case are entirely reasonable, given two round trips and a commit against real software. Our unit suite still finishes in under a second, so nobody waits on Docker while writing logic. Both suites run in the pipeline from the previous chapter, though the integration job carries a longer timeout. We then treat convergence as our default assertion for anything touching a device.

Canary, Verify and Roll Back

Staging Fleet Change

A change correct on two switches can still be wrong on six hundred. After all, vendors differ, firmware differs, and one region invariably carries a configuration nobody documented. Our defence is a wave schedule, where we apply to a small canary group, verify a health gate, and only then widen. Each wave grows geometrically, so a fault reaches a handful of devices rather than the whole estate. Nothing about this is sophisticated, and very little else protects us as well.

In the following, we can envisage the rollout as a state machine prior to its implementation:

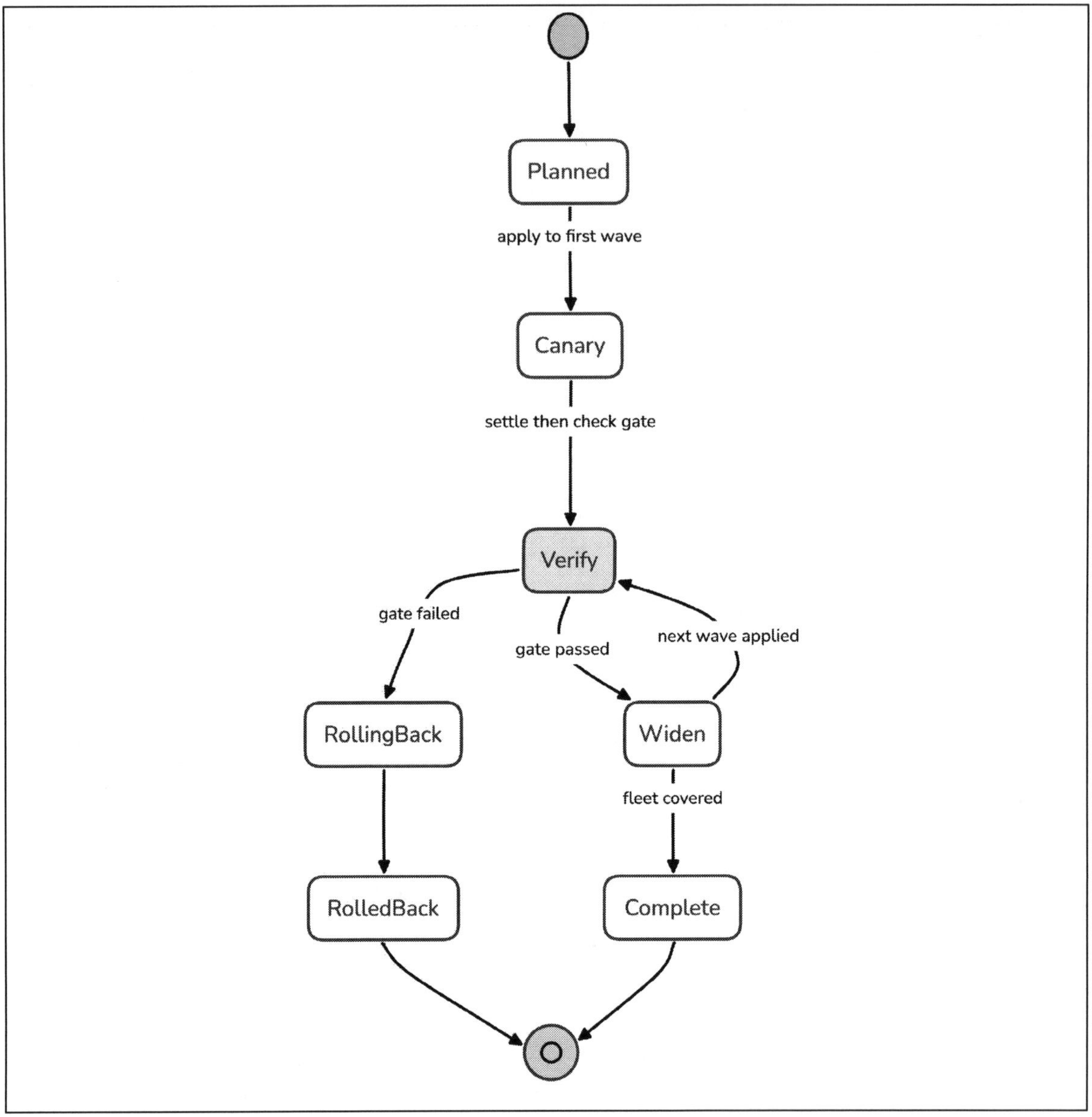

Our health gate deserves as much thought as the change itself. A gate checking only that the commit succeeded proves almost nothing, since a device happily commits a configuration which breaks its own adjacencies. We therefore gate on observable behaviour, meaning interface state, neighbour sessions, and error rates read back after a settling delay. The next chapter gives us the model-driven reads which make such gates precise.

In the following script, we will implement the wave loop with a gate between every widening:

```
Result<void> rollout(std::span<const Device> fleet,
                     const DesiredState& want,
```

```
                    Gate& gate,
                    Executor& exec) {
    std::size_t start = 0;
    std::size_t wave = 1;

    while (start < fleet.size()) {
        const auto slice = fleet.subspan(
            start, std::min(wave, fleet.size() - start));

        for (const Device& d : slice) {
            auto plan = plan_for(d, want, transport_for(d));
            if (!plan) {
                return std::unexpected(plan.error());
            }
            if (auto applied = exec.apply(*plan); !applied) {
                return roll_back(fleet.first(start + slice.size()),
want);
            }
        }

        std::this_thread::sleep_for(std::chrono::seconds(30));
        if (auto healthy = gate.check(slice); !healthy) {
            std::println("netops: gate failed on wave of {}",
slice.size());
            return roll_back(fleet.first(start + slice.size()),
want);
        }

        start += slice.size();
        wave *= 4;
    }
    return {};
}
```

Our wave grows by a factor of four each time, so a fleet of six hundred devices clears in six waves rather than in six hundred steps. The gate runs between every widening, and a failure at any point reverses everything applied so far rather than only the slice which failed. That thirty-second sleep is deliberate rather than lazy, because an interface which has just come up reports itself healthy for a moment before its adjacencies settle. We will replace the fixed delay in the next chapter, where a device can tell us when it is genuinely ready.

Automatic Rollback on Failed Gate

Any reversal works only when we captured the previous state before changing anything. Our plan already holds the observed value for every step, which happens to be exactly the information a reversal needs. We therefore keep applied plans in memory for the duration of a rollout and invert them the moment a gate fails. An inverted step swaps desired and observed, while a step which created a path becomes a step which removes it.

So here, we will write the inversion which makes rollback possible:

```
ChangePlan invert(const ChangePlan& plan) {
    ChangePlan back{.device = plan.device};
    for (const Step& s : plan.steps) {
        if (s.action == Action::none) {
            continue;
        }
        Step r{.path = s.path, .desired = s.observed, .observed =
s.desired};
        r.action = (s.action == Action::create) ? Action::remove :
Action::update;
        back.steps.push_back(std::move(r));
    }
    return back;
}
```

Once a gate fails on the second wave, our tool reverses everything it applied and stops.

```
netops: wave 1 applied to srl1, gate passed after 30 s
netops: wave 2 applied to srl2, gate failed
netops: gate failed on wave of 1
netops: rolling back 2 devices
netops: srl2 reverted, srl1 reverted
netops: rollout aborted, fleet left at previous state
```

No reversal is ever entirely free, and we would mislead ourselves badly by pretending otherwise. A device which rejected our edit may also reject the reversal, and a configuration which broke a neighbour session may prevent us from reaching the device at all. We therefore keep waves small enough that manual recovery stays feasible, and we write every applied plan to disk before applying it. Our rollout aborts on the first failed gate rather than continuing hopefully. None of this exists to make change faster, because the real gain is that our recovery gets written before the risk is ever taken.

Summary

We have now given **netops** a discipline rather than merely another capability. Our change plans separate deciding from doing, so a preview exercises the same decisions a real run would make and cannot drift away from it. A converged device receives nothing at all, and a test proves that rather than a comment claiming it. The GoogleTest suite covers our pure logic in under a second, while fake transports turn unreproducible failures into ordinary cases.

The integration tests then checked our assumptions against real switches by asserting convergence rather than reply formats, which keeps them stable across firmware upgrades. Our rollout applies changes in growing waves behind a health gate, and it inverts every applied plan the moment that gate fails. In the next chapter, we replace the string paths in our desired state with model-driven ones, because NETCONF and YANG let a device validate our intent before it ever commits.

CHAPTER 4

DEVICE CONFIGURATION WITH NETCONF, YANG AND gNMI

Our tool can plan, preview, test, and reverse a change, yet it still pushes configuration as opaque strings over a socket. A device deserves better than that, and so do we. This chapter replaces those strings with models the device itself understands, so a mistake gets caught by a schema rather than by an outage. Here, NETCONF supplies the transaction, YANG supplies the vocabulary, and gNMI supplies the telemetry which closes our health gate.

In this chapter, we will build a NETCONF session class, filtered reads against the running datastore, and a two-phase edit through the candidate datastore. Our plans then pass through libyang before they ever leave the process, which turns a whole class of failure into an early rejection. A gNMI subscription follows, feeding the **`Gate`** we deliberately left unimplemented in the previous chapter.

Model-Driven Configuration changes Everything

Cost of Screen Scraping

A great deal of network automation still sends command lines and parses whatever comes back. Such an approach works until it does not, and the failure mode is always the same. A vendor reflows a table by one column, and forty regular expressions stop matching on a Tuesday morning. Nothing in the transaction tells us whether a command actually succeeded, since a prompt returns identically for a rejected command and an accepted one. We inherit the whole burden of interpretation, and we carry it forever.

Two further costs hide behind the obvious one. A command line has no schema, so nothing prevents us from sending a value the device will reject after we have already changed six hundred others. Such partial application then becomes our normal state rather than an exception we handle. We also lose any notion of a transaction, because most command lines apply immediately and individually.

YANG, OpenConfig and Shared Vocabulary

A YANG module describes configuration and state as a typed tree, with constraints the device itself enforces. Every leaf carries a type, a range, and often a **`must`** expression tying it to another leaf. Our intent then becomes data rather than syntax, and data can be validated before it ever travels. The device publishes its modules, so we never guess at what a path means or which values it will accept.

The OpenConfig sits above the vendor modules as a neutral set, and it matters for one reason above all others. A path such as **`/interfaces/interface[name=ethernet-1/2]/config/description`** means the same thing on **`SR Linux`**, on **`Junos`**, and on **`Arista`**. Our desired state therefore survives a hardware refresh, which no command-line script has ever managed. The native modules remain available wherever OpenConfig lacks coverage, and we mix the two without any difficulty. We owe ourselves honesty about that coverage as well, since vendor support varies by platform and by release, and a path present in the documentation is occasionally absent from the firmware. Our approach in this book therefore reads the modules a device actually advertises rather than trusting a specification. The next chapter applies the same scepticism to server configuration, where the equivalent gap appears between a package version and its documented options.

NETCONF Sessions from C++

How Session Behaves?

Every NETCONF session follows a fixed lifecycle, and our code becomes simpler once we respect each stage of it. The client opens an SSH channel to port **`830`**, after which both sides announce capabilities through a **`<hello>`** message. Once that greeting completes, the session accepts remote procedure calls until either side closes it. Those capabilities matter more than they first appear, because they tell us which datastores exist. A device advertising **`:candidate`** lets us stage a change and inspect it before anything goes live.

The message identifiers deserve a moment as well. Each RPC we send carries a number, and every reply carries the number of the request which produced it. The library tracks those for us, yet it hands them back so we can correlate replies under concurrency. Our poller already runs coroutines across many devices at once. We will therefore keep one session for each device and never share a session between coroutines.

Let us now visualize that lifecycle before committing any of it to code:

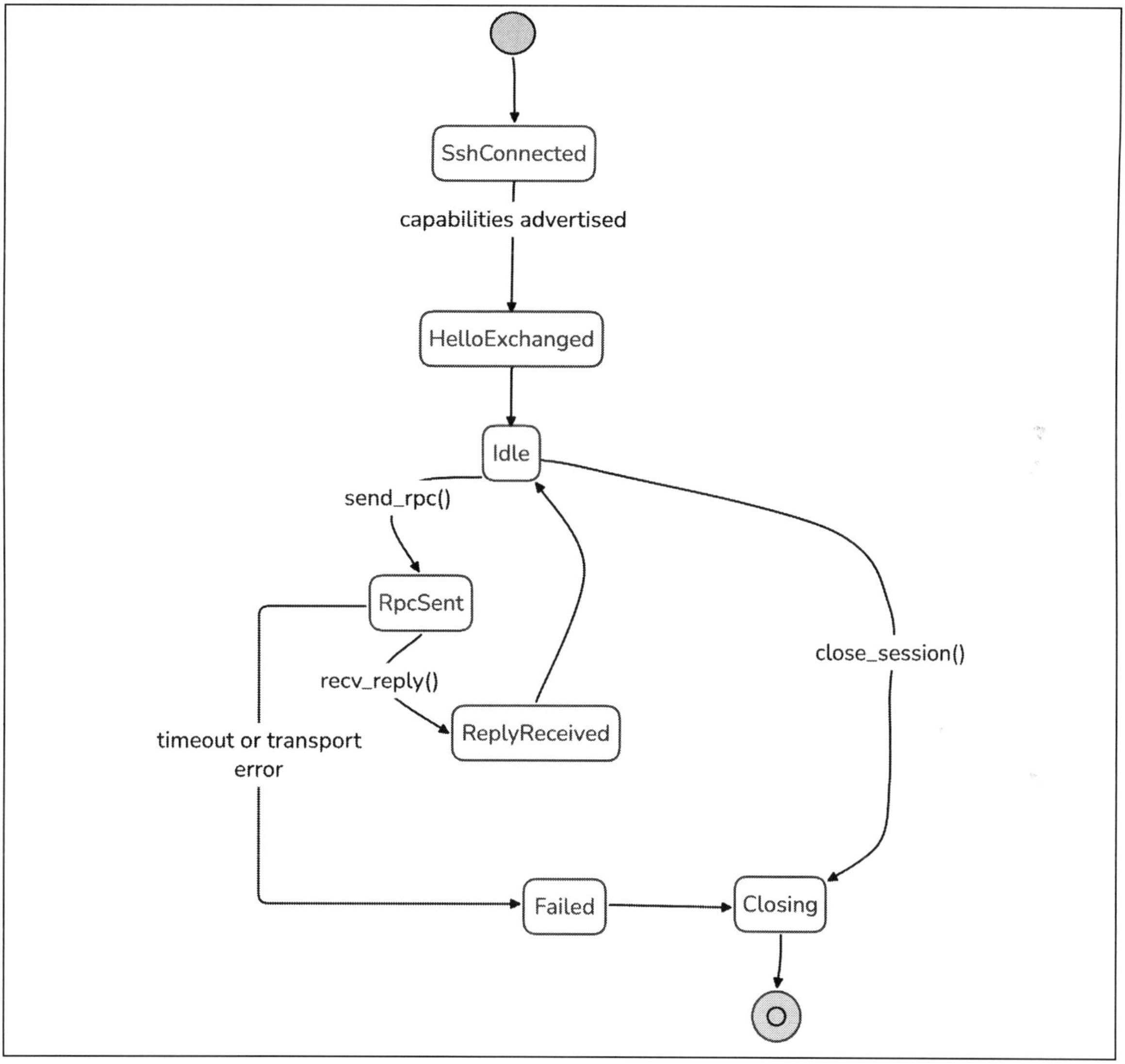

Opening Session with 'libnetconf2'

We will now add a **`netconf::Session`** class which wraps the raw handle and releases it exactly once. Our constructor stays private, and a static **`connect()`** factory hands back a **`Result`** rather than throwing. Those ownership rules matter here, because **`libnetconf2`** frees the handle once and a second free surfaces at three in the morning. Anybody using the class sees three operations and never a raw XML string.

In the following script, we will declare the class, delete the copy operations, and expose the operations our planner needs:

```
#pragma once
#include <netops/error.hpp>
#include <libnetconf2/netconf.h>
#include <libnetconf2/session_client.h>
#include <string>
#include <vector>

namespace netops::netconf {

class Session {
public:
    static Result<Session> connect(const std::string& host,
                                   uint16_t port,
                                   const std::string& user);

    Session(Session&& other) noexcept;
    Session& operator=(Session&& other) noexcept;
    Session(const Session&) = delete;
    Session& operator=(const Session&) = delete;
    ~Session();

    Result<std::string> get_config(const std::string& filter = {});
    Result<void> edit_candidate(const std::string& xml);
    Result<void> validate();
    Result<void> commit();

    const std::vector<std::string>& capabilities() const { return
caps_; }

private:
    explicit Session(nc_session* raw);
    Result<void> dispatch(nc_rpc* rpc, std::string_view label);

    nc_session* raw_ = nullptr;
    std::vector<std::string> caps_;
};

}
```

We can now write the factory, which brings the client library up exactly once for the whole process:

```
Result<Session> Session::connect(const std::string& host,
                                 uint16_t port,
                                 const std::string& user) {
```

```
    static std::once_flag init_once;
    std::call_once(init_once, [] { nc_client_init(); });

    nc_client_ssh_set_username(user.c_str());
    nc_session* raw = nc_connect_ssh(host.c_str(), port, nullptr);
    if (raw == nullptr) {
        return fail(Category::transport, ECONNREFUSED,
                    std::format("ssh session refused by {}",
host));
    }
    return Session(raw);
}
```

Once we point the binary at the fabric from the previous chapter, the device introduces itself before any work begins.

```
netops: connected to 172.20.20.11:830
netops: 41 capabilities advertised
netops:   urn:ietf:params:netconf:capability:candidate:1.0
netops:   urn:ietf:params:netconf:capability:rollback-on-error:1.0
netops:   urn:ietf:params:netconf:capability:validate:1.1
```

Those three lines decide how the rest of our component behaves. With **:candidate** and **:rollback-on-error** both present, we know the device will stage a change and undo it cleanly on failure. A device lacking either one receives a direct write instead, and our report says so plainly rather than pretending the safety net existed.

From here, we will start that alternative server for anybody preferring a lighter fabric:

```
docker run -d --name netopeer2 --network host \
    sysrepo/sysrepo-netopeer2:latest

./build/debug/netops --inventory lab/netopeer2.csv --dry-run
```

The Netopeer2 announces a smaller capability set, and our tool adapts to it without a single change on our side.

```
netops: connected to 127.0.0.1:830
netops: 18 capabilities advertised
netops:   urn:ietf:params:netconf:capability:candidate:1.0
netops:   urn:ietf:params:netconf:capability:validate:1.1
netops: rollback-on-error absent, direct write path selected
```

There are some eighteen capabilities against forty-one, which is the whole reason we read them rather than assume them. Our tool found **:candidate** and **:validate**, missed **:rollback-**

on-error, and selected the **direct write path** without anybody editing a configuration file. A run against this lighter server therefore exercises the same code as a run against SR Linux, and the report states plainly which safety net was available on the day.

Reading and Editing Datastores

Filtered Reads Aaainst Running

Our reads come first, since every safe change begins with an honest picture of the present. The **get-config** operation accepts a datastore name and an optional subtree filter, and it returns an XML document. Without a filter, a mid-sized router hands back several megabytes and buries the handful of nodes we cared about. Our **DesiredState** already knows which paths it needs, so the filter follows from the plan rather than from a guess.

In the following script, we will implement the read and serialize the reply into a string our parser can walk:

```
Result<std::string> Session::get_config(const std::string& filter)
{
    nc_rpc* rpc = nc_rpc_getconfig(NC_DATASTORE_RUNNING,
                                   filter.empty() ? nullptr :
filter.c_str(),
                                   NC_WD_ALL, NC_PARAMTYPE_CONST);
    uint64_t msgid = 0;
    if (nc_send_rpc(raw_, rpc, 2000, &msgid) != NC_MSG_RPC) {
        nc_rpc_free(rpc);
        return fail(Category::transport, EIO, "get-config could not
be sent");
    }

    lyd_node* envp = nullptr;
    lyd_node* op = nullptr;
    nc_recv_reply(raw_, rpc, msgid, 5000, &envp, &op);
    nc_rpc_free(rpc);

    char* buffer = nullptr;
    lyd_print_mem(&buffer, op, LYD_XML, LYD_PRINT_WITHSIBLINGS);
    std::string result = buffer ? buffer : "";
    free(buffer);
    lyd_free_tree(envp);
    lyd_free_tree(op);
    return result;
}
```

In that listing, two timeouts appear, and each one guards against a different failure. The send timeout of two seconds catches a wedged transport quickly, so we never wait on a session which will never reply. By contrast, the receive timeout of five seconds deliberately allows a slow control plane some room, because a device under heavy BGP churn routinely takes three seconds to serve a filtered read. A tighter value would manufacture failures across a fleet, and false alarms erode trust in a tool faster than almost anything else.

Candidate, Validate and Commit

The writes follow a different discipline, and the whole difference lies in giving ourselves a way back. Our edit lands in the candidate datastore first, where the device stores it and applies nothing. A separate **validate** RPC then asks the device to check that candidate against its own schema and cross-references. Only once both steps succeed do we commit, and only then does the change become real.

So here, we will then implement the three write operations through one shared dispatcher:

```
Result<void> Session::edit_candidate(const std::string& xml) {
    nc_rpc* rpc = nc_rpc_edit(NC_DATASTORE_CANDIDATE,
                              NC_RPC_EDIT_DFLTOP_MERGE,
                              NC_RPC_EDIT_TESTOPT_TESTSET,
                              NC_RPC_EDIT_ERROPT_ROLLBACK,
                              xml.c_str(), NC_PARAMTYPE_CONST);
    return dispatch(rpc, "edit-config");
}

Result<void> Session::validate() {
    nc_rpc* rpc = nc_rpc_validate(NC_DATASTORE_CANDIDATE, nullptr,
                                  NC_PARAMTYPE_CONST);
    return dispatch(rpc, "validate");
}

Result<void> Session::commit() {
    nc_rpc* rpc = nc_rpc_commit(0, 0, nullptr, nullptr,
NC_PARAMTYPE_CONST);
    return dispatch(rpc, "commit");
}
```

Our choice of **NC_RPC_EDIT_TESTOPT_TESTSET** repays a closer look. That option asks the device to validate the candidate and then apply it, which spares us a round trip on platforms honouring it. A device which cannot honour the option falls back to plain **set** behaviour, and the capability check from earlier catches that case before the RPC leaves us. We keep the explicit **validate()** call regardless, because a device-side check catches cross-leaf constraints which no local schema pass can see. Those three RPCs for one change look wasteful until the first time they save an estate, since a rejected candidate costs us four hundred milliseconds and changes nothing, whereas a rejected direct write leaves a device in a state nobody planned. Our previous chapter built waves and rollback for exactly the failures this pattern prevents, and neither defence makes the other redundant.

Validating Intent with 'libyang'

Loading Schema Context

A schema context is the in-memory picture libyang keeps of the modules we care about. We build it once at startup, load the modules the device advertised, and then keep it for the life of the process. That construction costs perhaps two hundred milliseconds, while every reuse costs nothing at all. Our validation therefore happens locally, at memory speed, with no round trip to any device.

We will now wrap that context in a small class which owns and releases it properly:

```
class SchemaContext {
public:
    static Result<SchemaContext> load(const
std::vector<std::string>& modules,
                                       const char* search_dir) {
        ly_ctx* raw = nullptr;
        if (ly_ctx_new(search_dir, LY_CTX_ALL_IMPLEMENTED, &raw) !=
LY_SUCCESS) {
            return fail(Category::internal, ENOMEM,
                        "libyang context could not be created");
        }

        SchemaContext ctx(raw);
        for (const std::string& m : modules) {
            if (ly_ctx_load_module(raw, m.c_str(), nullptr,
nullptr) == nullptr) {
                return fail(Category::validation, ENOENT,
                            std::format("module '{}' absent from
{}", m, search_dir));
            }
        }
        return ctx;
    }

    ly_ctx* raw() const { return ctx_.get(); }

private:
    explicit SchemaContext(ly_ctx* c) : ctx_(c, ly_ctx_destroy) {}
```

```
    std::unique_ptr<ly_ctx, void (*)(ly_ctx*)> ctx_;
};
```

Here, two sources supply those modules, and the choice between them matters operationally. A device advertising **:yang-library** serves its own schemas over NETCONF, which guarantees an exact match with the running firmware. Anything older forces us onto a local directory of **.yang** files, where a mismatch between our copy and the device becomes possible. We prefer the device-served path and log loudly whenever we fall back, since a stale local schema validates a plan the device will later reject.

Rejecting Bad Plan In-Advance

The local validation changes the economics of a fleet run entirely. A typo in a leaf name currently costs us six hundred round trips and a partial application, whereas libyang catches the same typo in microseconds before the first socket opens. We therefore validate the whole plan as a pre-flight step, and we refuse to start whenever any single step fails. Nothing reaches the network until every device's plan has passed.

We then proceed to build a data tree from the plan and validate it against the schema:

```
Result<void> validate(const SchemaContext& ctx, const ChangePlan&
plan) {
    lyd_node* tree = nullptr;

    for (const Step& s : plan.steps) {
        if (s.action == Action::none) {
            continue;
        }
        const LY_ERR rc = lyd_new_path(tree, ctx.raw(),
s.path.c_str(),
                                       s.desired.c_str(), 0,
&tree);
        if (rc != LY_SUCCESS) {
            const std::string detail = ly_last_errmsg();
            lyd_free_all(tree);
            return fail(Category::validation, EINVAL,
                        std::format("{} rejected at {} ({})",
                                    plan.device, s.path, detail));
        }
    }

    const LY_ERR rc = lyd_validate_all(&tree, ctx.raw(),
                                       LYD_VALIDATE_PRESENT,
nullptr);
    lyd_free_all(tree);
```

```
    if (rc != LY_SUCCESS) {
        return fail(Category::validation, EINVAL,
                    std::format("{} failed schema validation ({})",
                                plan.device, ly_last_errmsg()));
    }
    return {};
}
```

Once somebody sets an MTU beyond what the model permits, the run stops before a single session opens.

```
netops: pre-flight validation failed
  srl1  /interfaces/interface[name=ethernet-1/2]/config/mtu
        value "90000" out of range (1500..9500)
netops: 0 devices touched, plan rejected before dispatch
```

That final line is the one worth savouring. With zero devices touched, we face zero recovery work, zero partial state, and zero explaining to anybody. Our earlier rollback machinery remains ready for the failures which only a real device can reveal, while this check removes the failures we could have predicted. Both layers together give us a pipeline where the cheap check runs first.

We can also picture that pipeline end to end as below:

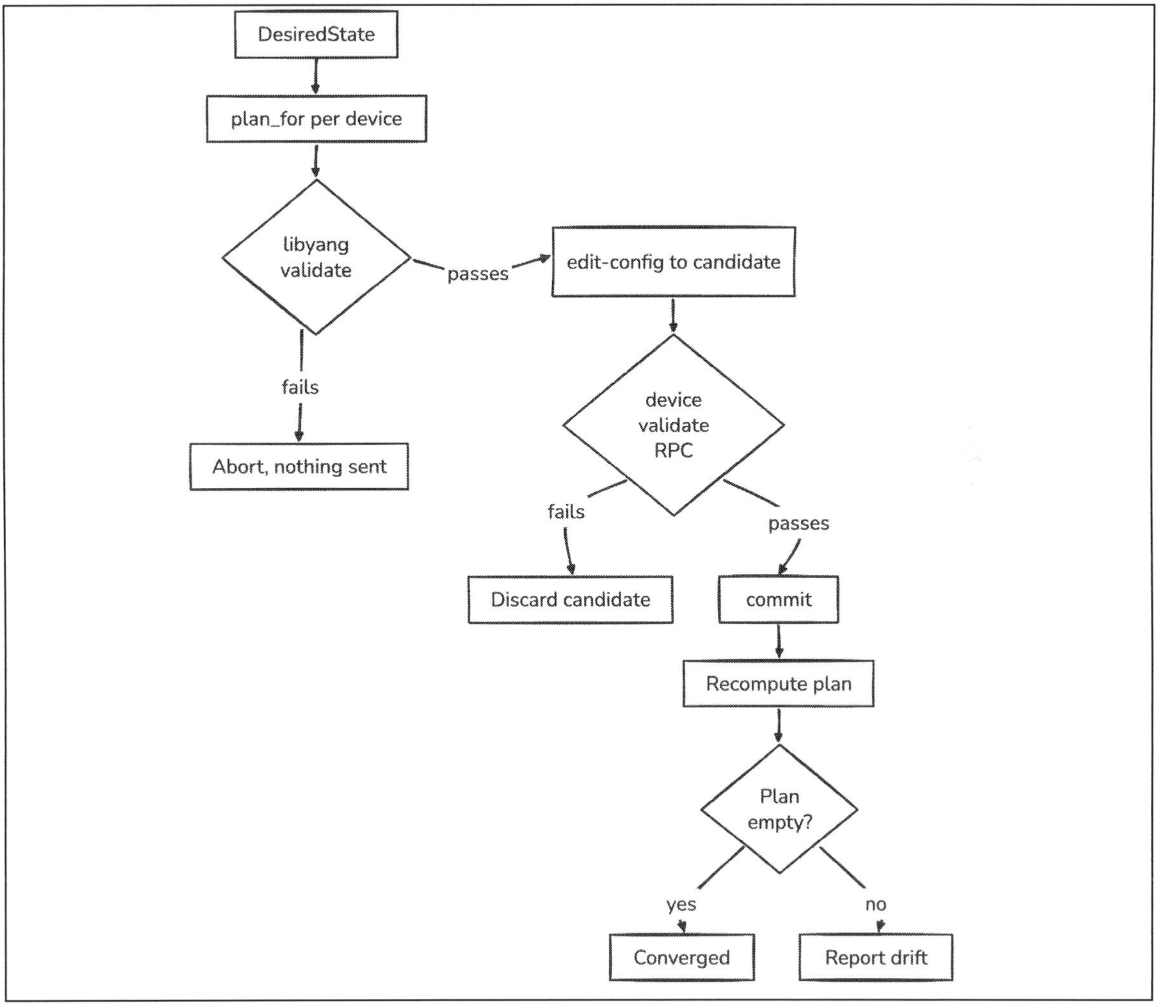

Streaming State with gNMI

gRPC Client for Subscribe

A poll tells us what a device looked like when we asked, while a stream tells us what it looks like now. That difference decides whether a health gate can work at all, because a gate polling once at thirty seconds misses a session which flapped at twenty. The gNMI protocol carries state over gRPC as protobuf messages, using the same OpenConfig paths our configuration already speaks.

Below, we will write a subscription client which streams sampled updates to a callback:

```
class GnmiClient {
public:
    GnmiClient(const std::string& target,
```

```
                std::shared_ptr<grpc::ChannelCredentials> creds)
        : stub_(gnmi::gNMI::NewStub(grpc::CreateChannel(target,
creds))) {}

    Result<void> subscribe(std::span<const std::string> paths,
                           std::chrono::seconds sample,
                           const std::function<void(const
gnmi::Notification&)>& on_update) {
        grpc::ClientContext ctx;
        auto stream = stub_->Subscribe(&ctx);

        gnmi::SubscribeRequest req;
        auto* sub = req.mutable_subscribe();
        sub->set_mode(gnmi::SubscriptionList::STREAM);
        for (std::string_view p : paths) {
            auto* s = sub->add_subscription();
            *s->mutable_path() = parse_path(p);
            s->set_mode(gnmi::SAMPLE);
            s->set_sample_interval(sample.count() *
1'000'000'000ULL);
        }
        if (!stream->Write(req)) {
            return fail(Category::transport, EIO, "subscribe
request rejected");
        }

        gnmi::SubscribeResponse resp;
        while (stream->Read(&resp)) {
            if (resp.has_update()) {
                on_update(resp.update());
            }
        }
        const auto status = stream->Finish();
        if (!status.ok()) {
            return fail(Category::transport, status.error_code(),
                        status.error_message());
        }
        return {};
    }

private:
    std::unique_ptr<gnmi::gNMI::Stub> stub_;
};
```

The sample mode appears there rather than on-change mode, and the choice is deliberate. An on-change subscription is ideal for interface state, while it behaves poorly for anything the device updates continuously. Our gate needs both kinds, so we sample the busy paths and subscribe on change to the quiet ones. We may mix the two inside one request quite legally, and such a mixture keeps our subscription list to a single stream for each device.

With that in place, we will trace one subscription through its lifetime:

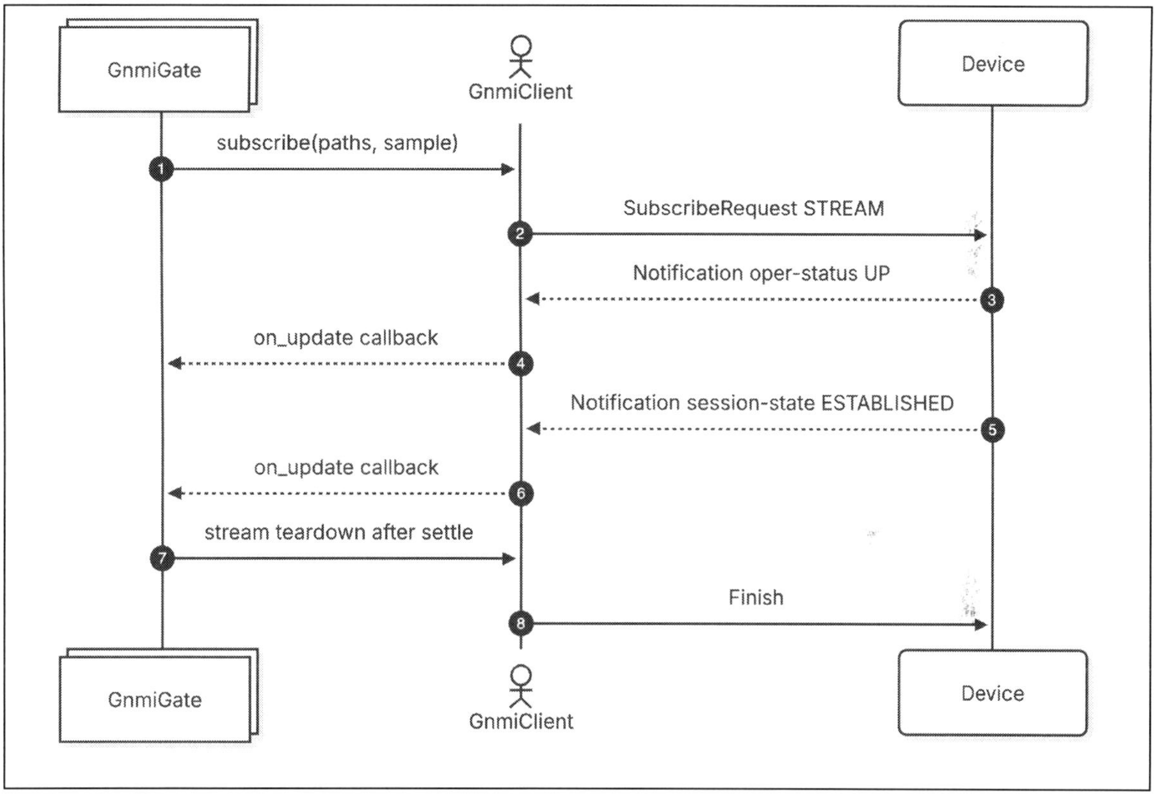

Turning Notifications into Health Gate

Our previous chapter declared a **Gate** interface and left it unimplemented, because a meaningful gate needs exactly what gNMI now gives us. A gate proving only that a commit succeeded proves very little, since a device happily commits a configuration which breaks its own adjacencies. We therefore check observable behaviour after a settling delay, meaning interface state and neighbour sessions rather than commit status.

We are now ready to implement the gate against those two path families:

```
class GnmiGate final : public Gate {
public:
    GnmiGate(GnmiClient& c, std::chrono::seconds settle)
        : client_(c), settle_(settle) {}
```

```
    Result<void> check(std::span<const Device> wave) override {
        std::this_thread::sleep_for(settle_);

        for (const Device& d : wave) {
            auto state = client_.get(d.address, {
                "/interfaces/interface/state/oper-status",
                "/network-instances/network-
instance/protocols/protocol/bgp"
                "/neighbors/neighbor/state/session-state"});
            if (!state) {
                return std::unexpected(state.error());
            }
            for (const auto& [path, value] : *state) {
                if (path.ends_with("oper-status") && value != "UP")
{
                    return fail(Category::validation, EIO,
                                std::format("{} reports {} at {}",
                                            d.name, value, path));
                }
                if (path.ends_with("session-state") && value !=
"ESTABLISHED") {
                    return fail(Category::validation, EIO,
                                std::format("{} session {} at {}",
                                            d.name, value, path));
                }
            }
        }
        return {};
    }

private:
    GnmiClient& client_;
    std::chrono::seconds settle_;
};
```

Once a wave lands, the gate waits and then reports what it saw rather than what it assumed.

```
netops: gate settling for 30 s on wave of 1
netops: srl1 /interfaces/interface[name=ethernet-1/2]/state/oper-
status = UP
netops: srl1 bgp neighbor 10.0.0.2 session-state = ESTABLISHED
netops: gate passed
```

That settling delay is the parameter people get wrong most often. About thirty seconds suits interface and BGP state on a small fabric, while an IS-IS reconvergence across a large one may want ninety. A gate checking too early reports failure on a session which was merely still forming, and such false failures trigger a rollback nobody needed. We therefore make the delay a property of the change rather than a constant in the code.

Bringing Back to Netops

NetconfTransport behind Transport Interface

Our previous chapter promised a NETCONF implementation of the three-method **`Transport`** contract, and we can now supply it. The adapter holds a session, translates our paths into a subtree filter, converts a plan into an edit document, and forwards the commit. Nothing in the planner changes, because the planner never knew which transport it held. Our fake from the previous chapter therefore remains valid and continues to run in under a second.

At this point, we will write the adapter which joins the two halves of our tool:

```
class NetconfTransport final : public Transport {
public:
    static Result<NetconfTransport> open(const Device& d, const
std::string& user) {
        auto s = netconf::Session::connect(d.address, 830, user);
        if (!s) {
            return std::unexpected(s.error());
        }
        return NetconfTransport(std::move(*s));
    }

    Result<std::map<std::string, std::string>>
    read(const std::vector<std::string>& paths) override {
        return session_.get_config(subtree_filter(paths))
                       .and_then(parse_into_map);
    }

    Result<void> edit(const ChangePlan& plan) override {
        return session_.edit_candidate(to_xml(plan))
                       .and_then([this] { return
session_.validate(); });
    }

    Result<void> commit() override {
        return session_.commit();
    }

private:
```

```
    explicit NetconfTransport(netconf::Session s) :
session_(std::move(s)) {}
    netconf::Session session_;
};
```

Once we fold the **validate()** call into **edit()**, the two-phase discipline stays invisible to callers, which is exactly where it belongs. A planner asking to edit gets an edit which was checked, and no caller can forget the second step. Our **RealExecutor** from the previous chapter continues to work unmodified, since it still sees one edit followed by one commit. A small interface rewards us twice, once when we write it and again when the implementation arrives.

Whole Loop in One Run

We can now run the complete pipeline against the fabric, with schema validation ahead of dispatch and a gNMI gate behind the commit. In the following script, we will build, then apply with validation and the streaming gate both enabled:

```
cmake --build --preset debug
./build/debug/netops --inventory lab/devices.csv \
                     --desired lab/uplink.yaml \
                     --yang-dir /usr/share/yang/modules \
                     --apply --gate gnmi
```

Every stage now reports itself, and the summary tells us what actually moved.

```
netops: schema context loaded, 14 modules, 187 ms
netops: pre-flight validation passed for 2 devices
plan for srl1
  update   /interfaces/interface[name=ethernet-1/2]/config/enabled
false -> true
plan for srl2
  converged, no steps
netops: wave 1 applied to srl1, gate passed
netops: 2 devices, 1 changed, 1 converged, 0 failed, elapsed 41.7 s
```

That run of forty-one seconds looks slow for a single interface change, and almost all of it was the settling delay. Our schema load took under two hundred milliseconds, the plan and commit together took roughly one second, and the gate spent thirty seconds waiting on purpose. Yet speed was never the aim of this pipeline. We spent thirty seconds to avoid a change nobody noticed until morning, which is the bargain we strike with a device once it validates our intent as a colleague rather than as a target.

Summary

To sum up, we have replaced opaque strings with models on both directions of the wire. Our NETCONF session opens over SSH, reports its capabilities, and refuses to pretend a safety net exists when the device never advertised one. Meanwhile, filtered reads keep a fleet run affordable, while the candidate datastore plus an explicit validate RPC turn a risky push into a proposal we can withdraw. The libyang pre-flight then rejects a malformed plan in microseconds, leaving zero devices touched and zero recovery work.

Our gNMI client closed the last gap by streaming interface and neighbour state into the health gate the previous chapter had only declared. The **`NetconfTransport`** adapter finally joined both halves of the tool without the planner noticing anything, which is what a narrow interface buys us. In the next chapter, we carry the same declarative habit onto servers, where Ansible and direct SSH replace NETCONF and drift detection replaces the candidate datastore.

Chapter 5

Server Provisioning and Configuration Management

Our tool now configures network devices through models, transactions, and a schema which refuses bad intent. Yet servers offer us none of that comfort. A Linux host has no candidate datastore, no YANG module describing its packages, and no commit which either lands or does not. This chapter rebuilds the same safety from cruder parts, using declarative baselines, drift detection written in C++, and Ansible driven as an executor rather than trusted as a master.

We will now reach servers over libssh behind the very same **`Transport`** interface, collect observed facts, and report drift without silently repairing it. After that, Ansible arrives as one executor among several, with its check mode mapped onto the dry run we already built. Our patch waves reuse the rollout and the gate from earlier chapters, a compliance report closes the loop, and secrets stay out of our logs by design.

Servers without Candidate Datastore

What is Lost or Rebuilt?

A NETCONF device gave us three gifts, and a Linux host withholds all three. Nothing stages our change for inspection, nothing validates it against a schema, and nothing reverses it when one step of four fails. A package installs immediately, a sysctl applies the moment we write it, and a service restarts whether or not the next step will succeed. Our safety therefore has to come from how we sequence the work rather than from any protocol guarantee.

In their place, three substitutes carry most of that weight. We read the full observed state before deciding anything, we express intent as facts rather than commands, and we verify after applying rather than trusting an exit status. Such a loop is weaker than a transaction, and it is very much stronger than a shell script. We also keep waves small, because a partial failure across twelve servers is recoverable while the same failure across six hundred is a weekend.

Our next step is to place the two models side by side:

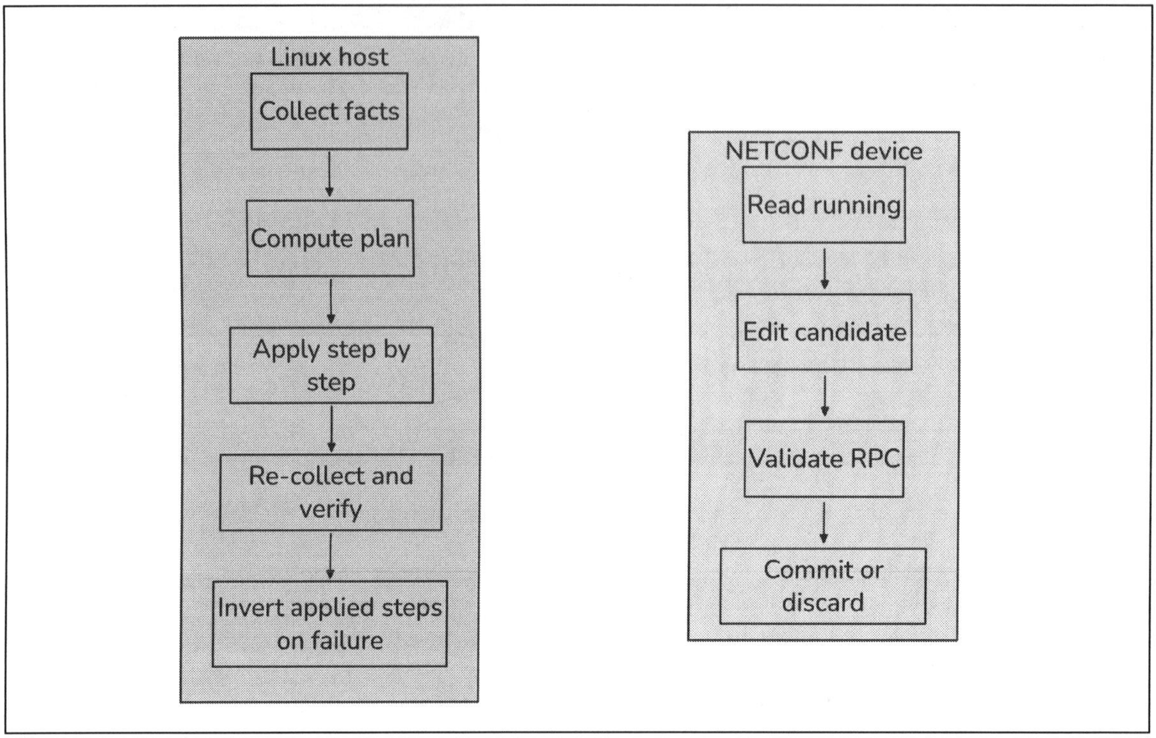

Baseline as Facts

A baseline names what must be true rather than what to run. Our file lists a package at a minimum version, a service in a state, a sysctl at a value, and a file with an owner and a mode. Nothing in it mentions **apt**, **systemctl**, or a playbook, so the same baseline describes a Debian host and a Rocky host alike. Our collectors then translate each fact into whatever probe the platform happens to need.

We will now write a baseline for our edge servers:

```
name: edge-server-baseline
version: 3

facts:
  - kind: package
    name: openssh-server
    min_version: "9.6p1"
  - kind: service
    name: sshd
    state: running
    enabled: true
  - kind: sysctl
    key: net.ipv4.tcp_syncookies
```

```
    value: "1"
  - kind: file
    path: /etc/ssh/sshd_config
    owner: root
    group: root
    mode: "0600"
  - kind: absent_package
    name: telnetd
```

That **`version`** field earns its line more than it first appears to. A baseline is a contract, and a contract which changes silently causes arguments nobody can settle. We bump the version with every edit, record it in the compliance report, and refuse to compare a report against a different version. Anybody asking why a server drifted last Tuesday then receives a precise reply rather than a shrug. Our fact kinds stay deliberately few for a related reason, since five kinds cover the overwhelming majority of what we assert across a fleet, and each new kind costs us a collector, a comparator, and a test. Somebody will eventually want a kind for firewall rules or for a mounted filesystem, and adding one takes an afternoon. We resist the temptation to model everything, because a baseline nobody can read stops being reviewed.

Reaching Servers over 'libssh'

Session, Channel and Exit Status

Every probe we run reduces to one pattern, namely a command, its output, and its exit status. The libssh library gives us all three, though it insists we manage the channel lifecycle carefully. Our wrapper opens a session once for each host, reuses it across probes, and closes it in a destructor. We reuse that session at fleet scale, because a fresh SSH handshake for every one of forty probes turns a two-second collection into eighty.

In the following script, we will declare the session and implement the command execution:

```
class SshSession {
public:
    static Result<SshSession> connect(const std::string& host,
                                      const std::string& user,
                                      const Credential& cred);

    struct Output {
        int status = -1;
        std::string out;
        std::string err;
    };

    Result<Output> run(std::string_view command);
```

```
    SshSession(SshSession&&) noexcept;
    SshSession(const SshSession&) = delete;
    ~SshSession();

private:
    explicit SshSession(ssh_session s) : s_(s) {}
    ssh_session s_ = nullptr;
};

Result<SshSession::Output> SshSession::run(std::string_view
command) {
    ssh_channel ch = ssh_channel_new(s_);
    if (ch == nullptr || ssh_channel_open_session(ch) != SSH_OK) {
        return fail(Category::transport, EIO, "channel could not be
opened");
    }

    Output o;
    if (ssh_channel_request_exec(ch, std::string(command).c_str())
!= SSH_OK) {
        ssh_channel_free(ch);
        return fail(Category::transport, EIO,
                    std::format("exec refused for '{}'", command));
    }

    char buf[4096];
    int n = 0;
    while ((n = ssh_channel_read(ch, buf, sizeof(buf), 0)) > 0) {
        o.out.append(buf, n);
    }
    while ((n = ssh_channel_read(ch, buf, sizeof(buf), 1)) > 0) {
        o.err.append(buf, n);
    }

    ssh_channel_send_eof(ch);
    o.status = ssh_channel_get_exit_status(ch);
    ssh_channel_free(ch);
    return o;
}
```

That exit status deserves more respect than most scripts give it. A probe returning zero with empty output usually means our command matched nothing rather than succeeding, and treating the two alike produces a compliance report full of false passes. Our collectors therefore assert on both the status and the shape of the output. We also capture standard error separately, since a sudo prompt on the error stream is the most common cause of a mysteriously empty result.

SshTransport behind Same Interface

Our **`Transport`** contract asked for three operations, and servers fit it with one honest compromise. Here, reads map cleanly onto probes, edits map onto a queued list of changes, and commit becomes the moment we actually apply that list. Nothing about a Linux host makes the commit atomic, so our implementation applies steps in order and stops at the first failure. The interface stays intact while the guarantee behind it weakens, and our report states that difference plainly.

Accordingly, we will write the adapter which puts servers behind the planner:

```
class SshTransport final : public Transport {
public:
    explicit SshTransport(SshSession s, const Platform& p)
        : ssh_(std::move(s)), platform_(p) {}

    Result<std::map<std::string, std::string>>
    read(const std::vector<std::string>& keys) override {
        std::map<std::string, std::string> observed;
        for (const std::string& k : keys) {
            auto probe = platform_.probe_for(k);
            auto o = ssh_.run(probe.command);
            if (!o) {
                return std::unexpected(o.error());
            }
            observed[k] = probe.parse(*o);
        }
        return observed;
    }

    Result<void> edit(const ChangePlan& plan) override {
        pending_ = plan;
        return {};
    }

    Result<void> commit() override {
        for (const Step& s : pending_.steps) {
            if (s.action == Action::none) {
                continue;
            }
            auto o = ssh_.run(platform_.command_for(s));
            if (!o || o->status != 0) {
                return fail(Category::protocol, EIO,
                            std::format("step {} failed with status
```

```
{}",
                                        s.path, o ? o->status : -
1));
            }
            applied_.push_back(s);
        }
        return {};
    }

    std::span<const Step> applied() const { return applied_; }

private:
    SshSession ssh_;
    const Platform& platform_;
    ChangePlan pending_;
    std::vector<Step> applied_;
};
```

That **`applied()`** accessor is what makes partial failure survivable. Our rollout from an earlier chapter inverts applied plans whenever a gate fails, and here it inverts only the steps which genuinely landed. A commit failing on step three of five therefore reverses two steps rather than five, which is the difference between a clean recovery and a fresh problem. A record of what happened costs us one vector and repays us on the first bad night.

Drift Detection in C++

Collecting Observed Facts

The drift we chase is the gap between a baseline and reality, and finding it is pure reading. Our collector runs one probe for each fact, parses the result, and records what it found beside what was wanted. Nothing changes during a collection, so we can run it hourly across a fleet with no approval process at all. Such freedom matters, because a drift report nobody fears becomes a drift report people actually read.

Now we will write the probe table which turns each fact kind into a read-only command:

```
Probe probe_for(const Fact& f, const Platform& p) {
    switch (f.kind) {
    case Kind::package:
        return {std::format("dpkg-query -W -f='${{Version}}' {}",
f.name),
                [](const SshSession::Output& o) { return
trim(o.out); }};
```

```
    case Kind::service:
        return {std::format("systemctl is-active {} 2>&1", f.name),
                [](const SshSession::Output& o) { return
trim(o.out); }};

    case Kind::sysctl:
        return {std::format("sysctl -n {}", f.key),
                [](const SshSession::Output& o) { return
trim(o.out); }};

    case Kind::file:
        return {std::format("stat -c '%U:%G:%a' {}", f.path),
                [](const SshSession::Output& o) { return
trim(o.out); }};

    case Kind::absent_package:
        return {std::format("dpkg-query -W {} >/dev/null 2>&1; echo
$?", f.name),
                [](const SshSession::Output& o) {
                    return trim(o.out) == "0" ? "present" :
"absent";
                }};
    }
    return {};
}
```

Each probe carries its own parser, and keeping the two together prevents a familiar bug. A command edited without its parser produces a value which compares wrongly rather than failing loudly, and such a fault survives review very easily. Our pairing makes the coupling visible in one place, and we keep every probe read-only by construction, so no collector can change a host even by accident. The platform differences hide inside **`Platform`** rather than inside our facts. A Debian host serves package queries through **`dpkg-query`**, while a Rocky host wants **`rpm -q`**, and neither detail belongs in a baseline somebody reviews. Our platform object resolves that at connection time from **`/etc/os-release`**. The next chapter uses the same separation when one control protocol carries several vendor dialects.

Reporting Drift without Fix

A collector which repairs what it finds is a collector nobody trusts to run. Our drift command therefore reports and stops, which lets us schedule it hourly and watch the trend. We keep remediation as a separate and deliberate act with its own approval and its own waves. Such separation also gives us something valuable, namely a history of how a fleet decays between changes.

We will now run a collection against twelve edge servers:

```
./build/debug/netops drift --inventory lab/servers.csv \
                          --baseline lab/edge-baseline.yaml
```

In the output below, four findings surface across three hosts, and the report puts wanted beside observed on every row.

```
drift against edge-server-baseline v3
host          fact                              wanted
observed
web-01        package openssh-server            >=9.6p1
9.2p1
web-01        sysctl net.ipv4.tcp_syncookies    1                 0
web-03        file /etc/ssh/sshd_config         root:root:0600
root:root:0644
db-02         absent_package telnetd            absent
present
netops: 12 hosts, 9 compliant, 3 drifted, 4 findings, elapsed 3.8 s
```

A report of four findings across three hosts stays readable, and readability was the entire design target. Our columns stay fixed so two reports diff cleanly, and the summary line lets a dashboard scrape one row rather than parse the whole thing. That **`telnetd`** finding on **`db-02`** is exactly the kind of decay which no change ticket ever mentions. Somebody installed a debugging tool in March and forgot it, and our hourly collection surfaced it without anybody asking.

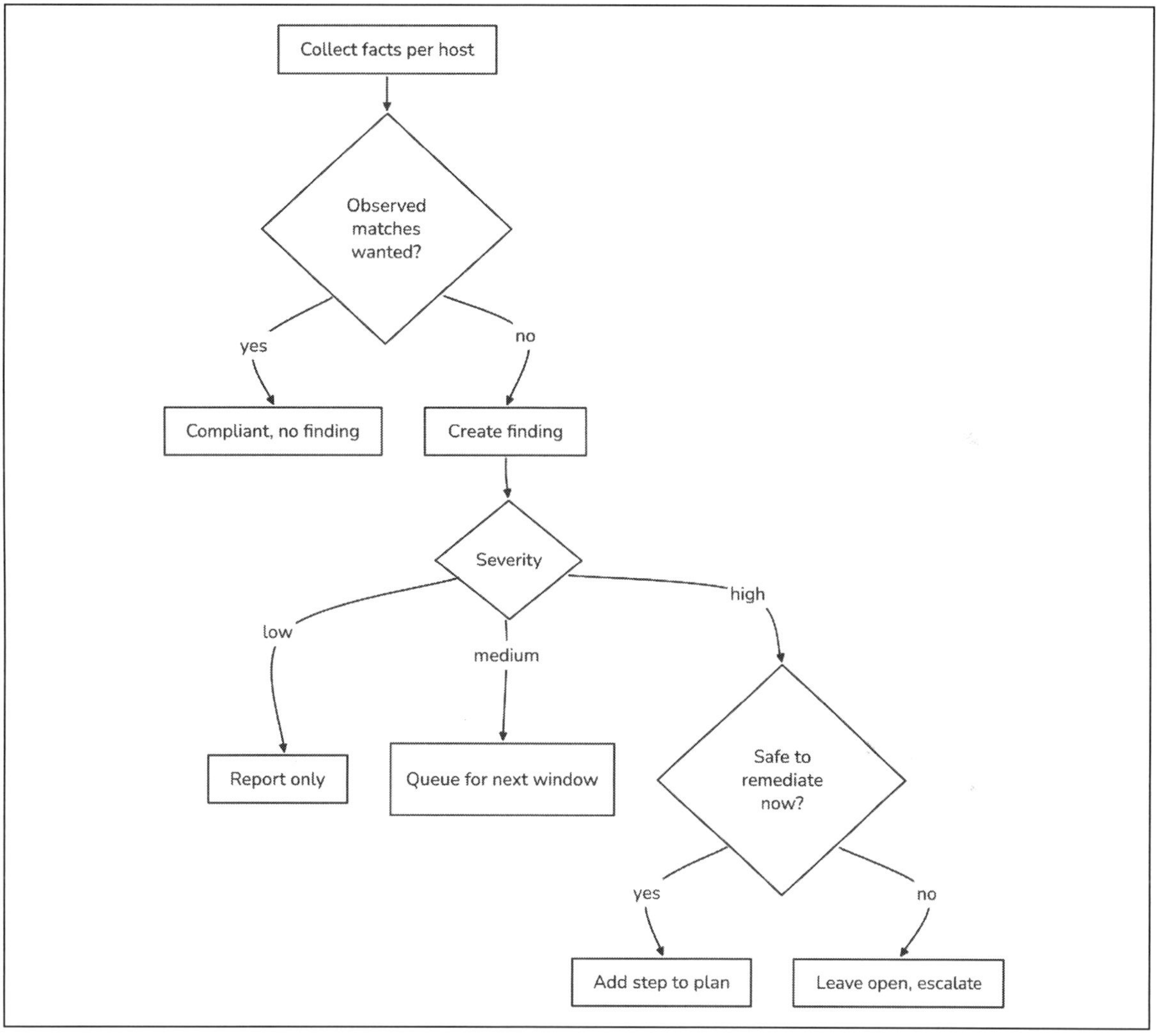

The above illustration shows us very wqell how the finding travels from collection to a decision.

Ansible as Executor

Driving a Playbook and Reading Its Result

The Ansible ecosystem earns its place through its module library rather than through its orchestration. Its thousands of well-tested modules already know how to install a package across nine distributions, and we would be foolish to rewrite that knowledge in C++. Our tool therefore keeps the deciding, the sequencing, the gating, and the reporting, while Ansible performs individual steps on request. Such a division plays to both strengths and avoids the usual trap of a C++ program which merely shells out. One detail makes the integration workable, namely the

JSON callback plugin. By default, Ansible prints prose intended for a person, which nobody should ever parse. With **ANSIBLE_STDOUT_CALLBACK=json**, we receive a structured document naming every task, host, and change, and our runner folds each task result back into our own **Step** records. A mixed run then reports uniformly whether a step came from Ansible or from a direct command.

In the following script, we will implement the executor which drives a playbook and reads its JSON result:

```
class AnsibleExecutor final : public Executor {
public:
    AnsibleExecutor(std::filesystem::path playbook, bool
check_mode)
        : playbook_(std::move(playbook)), check_(check_mode) {}

    Result<void> apply(const ChangePlan& plan) override {
        const auto cmd = std::format(
            "ANSIBLE_STDOUT_CALLBACK=json ansible-playbook {} "
            "--limit {} --extra-vars '{}' {}",
            playbook_.string(), plan.device, to_json(plan).dump(),
            check_ ? "--check" : "");

        auto out = run_local(cmd);
        if (!out) {
            return std::unexpected(out.error());
        }

        const auto doc = nlohmann::json::parse(out->out, nullptr,
false);
        if (doc.is_discarded()) {
            return fail(Category::internal, EPROTO,
                        "ansible json callback produced no
document");
        }

        for (const auto& play : doc["plays"]) {
            for (const auto& task : play["tasks"]) {
                const auto& host = task["hosts"][plan.device];
                if (host.value("unreachable", false)) {
                    return fail(Category::transport, EHOSTUNREACH,
                                std::format("{} unreachable",
plan.device));
                }
                if (host.value("failed", false)) {
                    return fail(Category::protocol, EIO,
                                std::format("{} failed at task '{}'
```

```
({})",
                                    plan.device,

task["task"]["name"].get<std::string>(),
                                    host.value("msg", "no
detail")));
                    }
                }
            }
        return {};
    }

private:
    std::filesystem::path playbook_;
    bool check_ = false;
};
```

That pair of failure branches is where most integrations go wrong. The Ansible run exits non-zero for a failed task and also for an unreachable host, and the two demand entirely different handling from us. An unreachable host belongs in the transport category and deserves a retry, while a failed task belongs in the protocol category and deserves a rollback. Our parser distinguishes them from the document rather than from the exit status.

Check Mode as Dry Run

As it happens, Ansible already carries a preview, and its name is check mode. The **`--check`** flag makes every well-written module report what it would change without changing anything, which maps exactly onto the dry run we built earlier. Our **`DryExecutor`** and **`AnsibleExecutor`** in check mode therefore serve the same purpose from two directions. Anybody previewing a mixed change sees one report covering both kinds of step.

To make that concrete, we will preview a remediation across the drifted hosts:

```
./build/debug/netops apply --inventory lab/servers.csv \
                           --baseline lab/edge-baseline.yaml \
                           --executor ansible --dry-run
```

As the following output shows, three steps appear across two hosts, and the module which would perform each one appears beside it.

```
plan for web-01
  update  package/openssh-server         9.2p1 -> >=9.6p1
[ansible: apt]
  update  sysctl/net.ipv4.tcp_syncookies  0 -> 1
[ansible: sysctl]
```

```
plan for web-03
  update  file//etc/ssh/sshd_config       0644 -> 0600
[ansible: file]
netops: check mode, 3 steps would change 2 hosts, nothing applied
```

One caveat belongs beside that convenience, since check mode is only as honest as the modules involved. A module built on **`command`** or **`shell`** cannot predict its own effect, so it reports a change it may not make or hides one it would. We therefore forbid those two modules inside any playbook our tool drives, and our loader rejects a playbook containing them. Such a rule is blunt, and it keeps our preview trustworthy.

Patching, Reboots and Compliance

Patch Waves with Health Gate

We treat patching as the most dangerous routine work we perform, because it changes everything at once and often demands a reboot. Our rollout from an earlier chapter already applies in growing waves behind a gate, so patching needs no fresh orchestration at all. What it does need is a gate suited to servers rather than to switches. A host which reboots must come back, rejoin its load balancer, and serve traffic before we widen.

Let us now write a gate which waits for a reboot and then for the services:

```
class ServiceGate final : public Gate {
public:
    ServiceGate(std::chrono::seconds settle,
std::vector<std::string> services)
        : settle_(settle), services_(std::move(services)) {}

    Result<void> check(std::span<const Device> wave) override {
        for (const Device& d : wave) {
            if (!wait_for_port(d.address, 22,
std::chrono::seconds(300))) {
                return fail(Category::timeout, ETIMEDOUT,
                            std::format("{} did not return from
reboot", d.name));
            }
        }
        std::this_thread::sleep_for(settle_);

        for (const Device& d : wave) {
            auto s = SshSession::connect(d.address, "netops",
credential_for(d));
            if (!s) {
```

```
                return std::unexpected(s.error());
            }
            for (const std::string& svc : services_) {
                auto o = s->run(std::format("systemctl is-active
{}", svc));
                if (!o || trim(o->out) != "active") {
                    return fail(Category::validation, EIO,
                                std::format("{} reports {} for {}",
d.name,
                                            o ? trim(o->out) :
"unknown", svc));
                }
            }
        }
        return {};
    }

private:
    std::chrono::seconds settle_;
    std::vector<std::string> services_;
};
```

Here, five minutes of patience for a reboot looks generous until a host runs a filesystem check. Our timeout therefore sits well above the normal case, while the settling delay stays short because services start quickly once SSH responds. Two waits with two different reasons beat one wait carrying a compromise value.

Compliance Report

A compliance report exists to be read by somebody who was not in the room. Our report therefore names the baseline and its version, lists every finding with its host and severity, and states plainly what was remediated and what remains. Nothing in it requires our tool to interpret anything. After all, most auditors ask the same four questions every year, and a report structured around those questions saves everybody a week.

We will now write the report as structured data rather than as prose:

```
Result<void> write_report(const std::filesystem::path& out,
                          const Baseline& base,
                          std::span<const Finding> findings) {
    nlohmann::json doc;
    doc["baseline"] = base.name;
    doc["baseline_version"] = base.version;
    doc["generated_at"] = iso8601_now();
    doc["hosts_total"] = hosts_in(findings);
```

```
    for (const Finding& f : findings) {
        doc["findings"].push_back({
            {"host", f.host},
            {"fact", f.fact},
            {"wanted", f.wanted},
            {"observed", f.observed},
            {"severity", to_string(f.severity)},
            {"state", f.remediated ? "remediated" : "open"}});
    }

    std::ofstream os(out);
    if (!os) {
        return fail(Category::internal, EIO,
                    std::format("report could not be written to
{}", out.string()));
    }
    os << doc.dump(2);
    return {};
}
```

Once the run finishes, our summary names the one finding which nobody may close automatically.

```
netops: report written to reports/edge-2026-08-17.json
netops: baseline edge-server-baseline v3
netops: 12 hosts, 4 findings, 3 remediated, 1 open
netops: open finding db-02 absent_package/telnetd severity=high
```

One open finding is not a failure of the run, and our summary says so without apology. Somebody must decide whether removing **`telnetd`** from a database host at midnight is wiser than removing it during a maintenance window. Our tool refuses to make that call, since automation which quietly deletes packages from production databases loses its welcome very quickly. We report, we recommend, and we then wait for a decision.

Handling Secrets without Leak

Source of Credentials

A credential committed to a repository is the most common serious mistake in automation, and it is entirely avoidable. Our tool never reads a password from its configuration, and it never accepts one on a command line where **`ps`** would expose it. A **`CredentialProvider`** interface supplies them instead, with implementations for an SSH agent, an environment variable, and a secrets manager. Each host record names which provider to use rather than carrying any material itself.

With this, we will declare that interface, including two of its implementations:

```
class CredentialProvider {
public:
    virtual ~CredentialProvider() = default;
    virtual Result<Credential> for_host(const Device& d) = 0;
};

class AgentProvider final : public CredentialProvider {
public:
    Result<Credential> for_host(const Device&) override {
        if (std::getenv("SSH_AUTH_SOCK") == nullptr) {
            return fail(Category::validation, ENOENT,
                        "SSH_AUTH_SOCK absent, agent unavailable");
        }
        return Credential{Credential::Kind::agent, {}};
    }
};

class VaultProvider final : public CredentialProvider {
public:
    explicit VaultProvider(std::string mount) :
mount_(std::move(mount)) {}

    Result<Credential> for_host(const Device& d) override {
        auto secret = fetch_secret(std::format("{}/hosts/{}",
mount_, d.name));
        if (!secret) {
            return std::unexpected(secret.error());
        }
        return Credential{Credential::Kind::password,
std::move(*secret)};
    }

private:
    std::string mount_;
};
```

Our agent provider comes first for a solid reason, since a forwarded agent means no secret ever reaches our process at all. A key which never enters our address space cannot leak out of it. The vault provider exists for cases where a password is unavoidable, such as an appliance without key support. We prefer the first path everywhere it works, and we log which provider served each host so an audit can verify the claim.

Keeping Secrets Safe

A secret in memory leaks through three ordinary doors. Our logs print it whenever somebody logs a whole request, a core dump captures it when the process crashes, and a shell history keeps it when it arrived on a command line. Each door closes with a small and specific measure rather than with any grand design. We take all three, because a leak through any one of them is equally embarrassing.

So here, we will then build a secret type which resists all three failures:

```
class Secret {
public:
    explicit Secret(std::string value) : value_(std::move(value)) {
        if (!value_.empty()) {
            ::mlock(value_.data(), value_.size());
        }
    }

    ~Secret() {
        if (!value_.empty()) {
            ::explicit_bzero(value_.data(), value_.size());
            ::munlock(value_.data(), value_.size());
        }
    }

    Secret(const Secret&) = delete;
    Secret& operator=(const Secret&) = delete;

    std::string_view expose() const { return value_; }

private:
    std::string value_;
};

template <>
struct std::formatter<netops::Secret> :
std::formatter<std::string_view> {
    auto format(const netops::Secret&, auto& ctx) const {
        return
std::formatter<std::string_view>::format("<redacted>", ctx);
    }
};
```

That formatter specialisation is the quietest and most useful line in the whole class. Any code path printing a **`Secret`** through **`std::print`** renders **`<redacted>`** rather than the value, so a careless log statement fails safe. The **`mlock`** call keeps the material out of swap, while **`explicit_bzero`** clears it on destruction without the compiler optimising the write away. We also disable core dumps in production through the systemd unit, since no mitigation inside our process survives a full memory image. Each measure is small on its own, and together they matter because a secret our own code cannot print beats a policy asking us not to print it.

Summary

We have now carried the declarative habit onto hosts which offer none of the protocol comforts. Our baseline names facts rather than commands, so one file describes a Debian host and a Rocky host alike. Every collection over libssh stays read-only by construction, and the drift command reports without repairing so nobody fears running it hourly. The **`SshTransport`** adapter kept our planner unchanged while recording exactly which steps landed.

By then, Ansible had joined us as an executor rather than a master, with its JSON callback folded into our own step records and its check mode serving as our preview. The patch waves reused the earlier rollout behind a gate which waits first for a reboot and then for the services. Our compliance report addresses the four questions auditors always ask, and secrets never reach a log or a core. In the next chapter, we turn toward software-defined networking, where one control protocol carries several vendor dialects.

CHAPTER 6
SOFTWARE-DEFINED NETWORKING WITH C++

Our tool has configured devices and servers by asserting state and then verifying it. Now, software-defined networking asks something slightly different of us, because the thing we configure is no longer a box. A controller, a virtual switch, and a proxy each hold part of the forwarding decision, and our work becomes assembling them into one coherent whole. This chapter keeps our planner exactly as it is and adds several new dialects behind it.

We will now write a JSON-RPC client for OVSDB, build VXLAN overlays through netlink rather than through shell commands, render flow tables declaratively, and configure Envoy and Istio as data. An intent model then sits above all of them, so one statement of what we want compiles down into several plans. Nothing here demands programmable hardware or a P4 pipeline.

What Software-Defined Actually Buys?

Separating Decision from Forwarding

A traditional switch decides and forwards inside the same chassis, which turns every policy question into a per-device question. Our earlier chapters lived with that arrangement and worked around it by pushing the same intent to many devices. A software-defined arrangement moves the deciding somewhere central and leaves the forwarding distributed. One policy statement then produces consistent behaviour without our tool visiting six hundred boxes individually.

Two practical gains follow, and neither one concerns speed. We gain a single place to ask what the network is doing, which shortens every enquiry from an afternoon to a query. We also gain the ability to express policy in terms of workloads rather than of ports, because the controller knows where a workload currently lives. Such indirection is the whole point, and it survives a virtual machine moving between hosts. We owe ourselves honesty about the cost here too, since a central controller becomes a single point of failure, and a controller outage turns a self-healing network into a static one. We therefore treat controller state as configuration worth backing up, and we verify the data plane independently of whatever the controller believes. Our verification habit from the previous chapter carries over completely unchanged.

Where Control Protocols Live

Just three protocols carry almost all traffic between a controller and a switch. The OpenFlow protocol programs forwarding tables, OVSDB manages the switch configuration itself, and netlink configures the kernel data path on each host. Each one occupies a different layer, and confusing them wastes a considerable amount of time. Our chapter keeps them separate throughout, because a fault in one looks nothing like a fault in another.

One honest limitation shapes everything which follows. No maintained C++ library speaks OpenFlow, since the once-popular options have been unmaintained for years now. Anybody writing a controller from scratch would spend weeks and learn protocol trivia rather than automation. We therefore program flows by orchestrating **`ovs-ofctl`**, which is the approach every production toolchain takes, and we spend our C++ effort where it genuinely pays. By contrast, OVSDB and netlink both suit us perfectly. The OVSDB server speaks JSON-RPC, which our existing JSON dependency already handles, while netlink is a kernel interface with stable C headers.

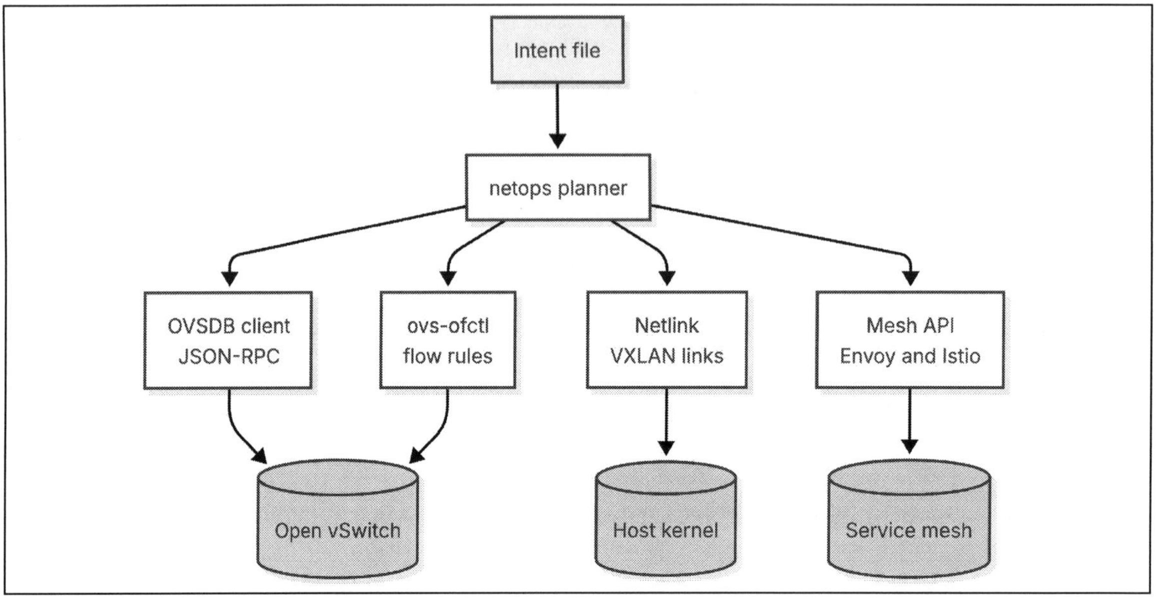

Our tool therefore owns switch configuration and the host data path directly, and it delegates only flow entry syntax to a mature command.

Talking OVSDB from C++

JSON-RPC Client over Management Socket

The OVSDB server listens on a Unix socket by default, and on TCP port 6640 whenever we ask it to. Both transports carry identical JSON-RPC messages, so our client cares only about framing. Every request carries a method, parameters, and an identifier, while a reply carries either a result or an error. Our existing JSON library handles the encoding and Boost.Asio handles the socket, which leaves us with roughly eighty lines of real work.

In the following script, we will implement the client and its single call method:

```
class OvsdbClient {
public:
    static Result<OvsdbClient> connect(const std::string& path);

    Result<nlohmann::json> call(std::string_view method,
                                const nlohmann::json& params) {
        nlohmann::json req{
```

```
            {"id", ++next_id_},
            {"method", method},
            {"params", params}};

        const std::string frame = req.dump();
        boost::system::error_code ec;
        boost::asio::write(sock_, boost::asio::buffer(frame), ec);
        if (ec) {
            return fail(Category::transport, ec.value(),
ec.message());
        }

        auto reply = read_one_object(sock_, buffer_);
        if (!reply) {
            return std::unexpected(reply.error());
        }

        const auto doc = nlohmann::json::parse(*reply, nullptr,
false);
        if (doc.is_discarded()) {
            return fail(Category::protocol, EPROTO, "malformed
ovsdb reply");
        }
        if (!doc.value("error", nlohmann::json()).is_null()) {
            return fail(Category::protocol, EINVAL,
doc["error"].dump());
        }
        return doc["result"];
    }

private:
    boost::asio::local::stream_protocol::socket sock_;
    std::string buffer_;
    std::uint64_t next_id_ = 0;
};
```

That **`read_one_object`** helper deserves a word, because OVSDB does not length-prefix its messages. A reply arrives as a bare JSON object, so we must track brace depth to know where it ends. Our helper reads until the depth returns to zero while ignoring braces which appear inside strings. Anybody tempted to search for a newline instead will discover that OVSDB sends none at all.

Bridges and Ports as a Change Plan

The OVSDB schema exposes tables rather than commands, which suits our declarative habit perfectly. A bridge is a row in **Bridge**, a port is a row in **Port**, and an interface is a row in **Interface**, with references linking the three. Our plan therefore becomes a set of insertions, mutations, and deletions inside one **transact** call.

```
Result<void> OvsdbClient::add_port(std::string_view bridge,
                                    std::string_view port,
                                    std::string_view type,
                                    const nlohmann::json& options) {
    const nlohmann::json params = nlohmann::json::array({
        "Open_vSwitch",
        {{"op", "insert"}, {"table", "Interface"},
         {"row", {{"name", port}, {"type", type}, {"options",
options}}},
         {"uuid-name", "iface"}},
        {{"op", "insert"}, {"table", "Port"},
         {"row", {{"name", port},
                  {"interfaces", nlohmann::json::array({"named-
uuid", "iface"})}}},
         {"uuid-name", "prt"}},
        {{"op", "mutate"}, {"table", "Bridge"},
         {"where", nlohmann::json::array({
             nlohmann::json::array({"name", "==", bridge})})},
         {"mutations", nlohmann::json::array({
             nlohmann::json::array({"ports", "insert",
                 nlohmann::json::array({"named-uuid",
"prt"})})})}}});

    return call("transact",
params).and_then(check_transact_errors);
}
```

With this, three operations now travel together, and the server reports on all of them at once.

```
netops: ovsdb transact on br-int
  insert Interface vxlan-to-host2 type=vxlan remote_ip=10.0.0.2
  insert Port      vxlan-to-host2
  mutate Bridge    br-int ports += prt
netops: transaction committed, 3 operations, 0 errors
```

Those **named-uuid** entries are the mechanism which makes one transaction possible. We insert an interface under a temporary name, reference that name from the port row, and reference the port from the bridge mutation. The server resolves all three at commit time. Without such naming, we would need three round trips with a partial state between each one, which is precisely the failure mode the previous chapter worked to avoid.

Building Overlays with Netlink

VXLAN Interfaces without Shelling Out

An overlay needs a tunnel endpoint on every host, and **`ip link add`** creates one perfectly well. Our tool nonetheless creates them through netlink directly, and the reason is not purity. A netlink request returns a structured error we can act upon, whereas a wrapped command returns a string we must parse and a status we must interpret. Our idempotency also becomes easier, since netlink tells us plainly whenever a link already exists.

With that in place, we will create a VXLAN endpoint and treat an existing one as success:

```
Result<void> ensure_vxlan(std::string_view name,
                          std::uint32_t vni,
                          const std::string& local,
                          const std::string& group,
                          std::uint16_t port) {
    nl_sock* sk = nl_socket_alloc();
    if (sk == nullptr || nl_connect(sk, NETLINK_ROUTE) < 0) {
        return fail(Category::internal, ENOMEM, "netlink socket
unavailable");
    }
    const std::unique_ptr<nl_sock, decltype(&nl_socket_free)>
guard(
        sk, nl_socket_free);

    rtnl_link* link = rtnl_link_vxlan_alloc();
    rtnl_link_set_name(link, std::string(name).c_str());
    rtnl_link_vxlan_set_id(link, vni);
    rtnl_link_vxlan_set_port(link, port);

    nl_addr* local_addr = nullptr;
    nl_addr_parse(local.c_str(), AF_INET, &local_addr);
    rtnl_link_vxlan_set_local(link, local_addr);

    nl_addr* group_addr = nullptr;
    nl_addr_parse(group.c_str(), AF_INET, &group_addr);
    rtnl_link_vxlan_set_group(link, group_addr);

    const int rc = rtnl_link_add(sk, link, NLM_F_CREATE |
NLM_F_EXCL);
    rtnl_link_put(link);

    if (rc == -NLE_EXIST) {
        return {};
```

```
    }
    if (rc < 0) {
        return fail(Category::protocol, -rc, nl_geterror(rc));
    }
    return {};
}
```

That **-NLE_EXIST** branch is our idempotency expressed in one line. A link already present produces success rather than an error, so a second run changes nothing and reports converged. We deliberately keep **NLM_F_EXCL** set rather than passing **NLM_F_REPLACE**, because replacing a live tunnel would drop traffic during a rerun. Our habit of reading before writing then covers the remaining case, where an existing link carries the wrong VNI.

Verifying Complete Overlay

A tunnel which exists is not a tunnel which works. Our verification therefore sends traffic rather than inspecting configuration, because almost every real overlay failure lives in the path rather than in the definition. An MTU mismatch, a blocked UDP port, or a missing underlay route each produce a healthy-looking link which carries nothing at all. We verify from inside the overlay, and we verify at the size which actually matters.

Accordingly, we will send full-size packets with fragmentation forbidden and inspect the datapath:

```
sudo ip netns exec ns-a ping -c 3 -M do -s 1422 10.200.0.2
sudo ovs-appctl dpif/dump-flows br-int | head -5
```

Both checks report together, and the second one proves where the encapsulation happened.

```
3 packets transmitted, 3 received, 0% packet loss, time 2003ms
recirc_id(0),in_port(2),eth(src=02:00:0a:c8:00:01),eth_type(0x0800)
,
  ipv4(frag=no), packets:3, bytes:1470, used:0.184s,

actions:set(tunnel(tun_id=0x64,dst=10.0.0.2,ttl=64,flags(df|key))),
1
```

There, two facts arrive together, and both of them matter. Our ping succeeded at 1422 bytes with fragmentation forbidden, which proves the underlay MTU tolerates a VXLAN header. The datapath dump then shows a real flow carrying a tunnel action, which proves the encapsulation happens in the kernel rather than in our hopes. We fold both checks into a **Gate** implementation, so an overlay change passes through the same wave discipline as everything else.

Flow Programming through 'ovs-ofctl'

Orchestration over Implementation

We decided earlier against writing an OpenFlow controller, and the decision deserves a fuller defence. A minimal controller means implementing the handshake, the message framing, the table feature negotiation, and the barrier semantics, none of which teaches us anything about automation. Every production toolchain reaches for **`ovs-ofctl`** or for a vendor agent instead. Our C++ effort belongs in deciding which flows should exist, not in the bytes which express them.

One rule keeps that orchestration honest. We never build a flow string by concatenating whatever arrived from a configuration file, since a malformed match silently installs a rule which matches everything. Our renderer instead accepts a typed **`FlowRule`** and emits the string itself, so every field passes a validator first. Such discipline turns a shell invocation into something much closer to a prepared statement.

Declarative Flow Tables

A flow table is a set, and sets diff cleanly. Our tool therefore reads the installed flows, computes the set we want, and emits only the additions and the removals. Nothing gets replaced wholesale, because a **`replace-flows`** against a live switch drops packets during the gap. Our plan then carries flow rules exactly as it carried interface leaves in earlier chapters, which means the preview and the rollback need no changes.

In the following script, we will render a rule and diff the wanted set against the installed one:

```
std::string render(const FlowRule& r) {
    std::string s = std::format("table={},priority={}", r.table,
r.priority);
    for (const auto& [field, value] : r.match) {
        s += std::format(",{}={}", field, value);
    }
    s += std::format(",actions={}", join(r.actions, ","));
    return s;
}

Result<ChangePlan> flow_plan(std::string_view bridge,
                             std::span<const FlowRule> wanted,
                             const OvsCommands& ovs) {
    auto installed = ovs.dump_flows(bridge);
    if (!installed) {
        return std::unexpected(installed.error());
    }
```

```
    ChangePlan plan{.device = std::string(bridge)};
    const auto have = std::ranges::to<std::set<std::string>>(
        *installed | std::views::transform(normalise));

    for (const FlowRule& r : wanted) {
        const auto rendered = render(r);
        if (!have.contains(normalise(rendered))) {
            plan.steps.push_back({.path = rendered, .desired =
"present",
                                  .action = Action::create});
        }
    }
    for (const std::string& existing : have) {
        if (!wanted_contains(wanted, existing)) {
            plan.steps.push_back({.path = existing, .observed =
"present",
                                  .action = Action::remove});
        }
    }
    return plan;
}
```

Our diff now reports two steps rather than reinstalling the whole table.

```
plan for br-int
  create
table=0,priority=200,ip,nw_dst=10.200.0.0/24,actions=output:vxlan-
to-host2
  remove  table=0,priority=100,ip,nw_dst=10.200.0.0/24,actions=drop
netops: 2 flow steps, 1 added, 1 removed, table 0 depth unchanged
```

That **`normalise`** function carries far more weight than its size suggests. The Open vSwitch dump reorders match fields and adds volatile ones such as **`cookie`** and **`duration`**, so a naive string comparison reports every flow as drifted. Our normaliser strips those fields and sorts the remainder, which makes the diff stable between dumps. Anybody skipping that step finishes with a tool which rewrites the entire table on every run.

Service Mesh Configuration as Data

Envoy Clusters and Routes

An Envoy proxy accepts configuration as data, which places it squarely inside our existing habits. Two paths exist, namely the admin interface for inspection and the **`xDS API`** for dynamic configuration. Our tool reads current clusters and listeners over the admin interface, computes a plan, and pushes the result through the control plane rather than writing files onto a proxy. The **Boost.Beast** library already carries our HTTP work, so no new dependency arrives with this section.

Once this is in place, we will read a configuration dump and parse it into something we can diff:

```
Result<nlohmann::json> EnvoyAdmin::config_dump(std::string_view
resource) {
    boost::beast::http::request<boost::beast::http::empty_body>
req{
        boost::beast::http::verb::get,
        std::format("/config_dump?resource={}", resource), 11};
    req.set(boost::beast::http::field::host, host_);

    boost::beast::http::write(stream_, req);

    boost::beast::flat_buffer buffer;
    boost::beast::http::response<boost::beast::http::string_body>
res;
    boost::beast::http::read(stream_, buffer, res);

    if (res.result() != boost::beast::http::status::ok) {
        return fail(Category::protocol,
static_cast<int>(res.result_int()),
                    std::format("admin interface returned {}",
res.result_int()));
    }

    const auto doc = nlohmann::json::parse(res.body(), nullptr,
false);
    if (doc.is_discarded()) {
        return fail(Category::protocol, EPROTO, "config_dump was
not valid JSON");
    }
    return doc;
}
```

One caution belongs with that admin interface, since it exposes secrets and accepts destructive requests. A reachable admin port is a serious finding in its own right, so the baseline from the previous chapter asserts that it binds to localhost only. We read through a local port forward rather than across the network. Our tool also refuses to issue any admin request beyond **config_dump** and the statistics endpoints.

Istio Resources

The Istio configuration arrives as declarative resources rather than as API calls, which suits us very well. A **VirtualService** describes routing, a **DestinationRule** describes load balancing and outlier detection, and both are ordinary documents. Our tool generates them from intent, validates them locally, and then diffs them against whatever the mesh currently holds. That generation and validation are where our C++ earns its place, since a malformed weight distribution is trivial to produce by hand.

We will now generate a routing resource and refuse it when the weights do not balance:

```
Result<nlohmann::json> virtual_service(const RouteIntent& intent) {
    int total = 0;
    for (const auto& dest : intent.destinations) {
        total += dest.weight;
    }
    if (total != 100) {
        return fail(Category::validation, EINVAL,
                    std::format("weights for {} sum to {}, expected
100",
                                intent.service, total));
    }

    nlohmann::json routes = nlohmann::json::array();
    for (const auto& dest : intent.destinations) {
        routes.push_back({{"destination",
                           {{"host", intent.service},
                            {"subset", dest.subset}}},
                          {"weight", dest.weight}});
    }

    return nlohmann::json{
        {"apiVersion", "networking.istio.io/v1"},
        {"kind", "VirtualService"},
        {"metadata", {{"name", intent.service}}},
        {"spec", {{"hosts",
nlohmann::json::array({intent.service})},
                  {"http", nlohmann::json::array({{{"route",
routes}}})}}}};
}
```

That weight check catches the single most common mesh mistake. A canary split of ninety and five leaves five percent of requests without a route, and the resulting behaviour depends on the Istio version rather than on our intent. Our validator refuses the document before it ever reaches the cluster, exactly as libyang refused a malformed device plan. Both checks share one shape, since a local rejection always beats a remote one.

Intent

Intent Model above Dialects

By now, four dialects sit behind our planner, and we would defeat the entire purpose by expressing the same policy four times. An intent file therefore names what we want in terms of workloads and reachability, with no mention of bridges, flows, or subsets. Our renderers then translate that intent into a plan for each layer. The previous chapter kept platform differences inside a **`Platform`** object, and this is the same separation applied one level higher.

We will now write an intent for one tenant, naming outcomes rather than tools:

```
name: tenant-blue
version: 2

segments:
  - name: blue-app
    vni: 100
    subnet: 10.200.0.0/24
    hosts: [host-a, host-b]

reachability:
  - from: blue-app
    to: blue-db
    ports: [5432]
    action: allow
  - from: blue-app
    to: any
    action: deny

traffic:
  - service: checkout.blue.svc
    destinations:
      - subset: v1
        weight: 90
      - subset: v2
        weight: 10
```

Nothing in that file names a tool, and the omission is entirely deliberate. A segment becomes a VXLAN link through netlink, a bridge port through OVSDB, and a set of flow rules through **`ovs-ofctl`**, while the traffic block becomes a **`VirtualService`**. Our intent therefore survives a change of implementation, which is the same durability OpenConfig gave us for device configuration.

One Intent and Several Renderers

Each renderer produces a **`ChangePlan`** and nothing else, which keeps our existing machinery completely intact. Our preview, validation, waves, gates, and rollback all continue working, because none of them ever learns which renderer produced a plan. Such uniformity is the quiet payoff of everything we built in earlier chapters. We could add a fifth dialect later for the price of one renderer and no changes anywhere else.

Our next step is to picture the compilation before we write it:

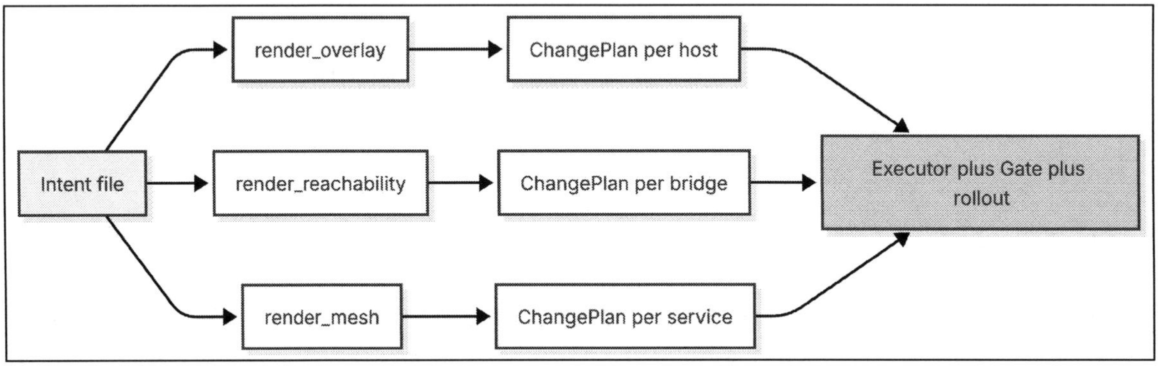

In the following script, we will compile one intent into a list of ordinary plans:

```
Result<std::vector<ChangePlan>> compile(const Intent& intent,
                                        const Fabric& fabric) {
    std::vector<ChangePlan> plans;

    for (const Segment& seg : intent.segments) {
        for (const std::string& host : seg.hosts) {
            auto p = render_overlay(seg, fabric.host(host));
            if (!p) {
                return std::unexpected(p.error());
            }
            plans.push_back(std::move(*p));
        }
    }

    auto flows = render_reachability(intent.reachability, fabric);
    if (!flows) {
        return std::unexpected(flows.error());
    }
    plans.insert(plans.end(), flows->begin(), flows->end());

    for (const RouteIntent& r : intent.traffic) {
        auto mesh = render_mesh(r);
        if (!mesh) {
```

```
            return std::unexpected(mesh.error());
        }
        plans.push_back(std::move(*mesh));
    }
    return plans;
}
```

We can now apply the whole intent behind the overlay gate:

```
sudo ./build/debug/netops sdn apply \
    --intent lab/tenant-blue.yaml \
    --fabric lab/fabric.yaml --gate overlay
```

Every dialect reports through the same plan format, and the summary closes the run.

```
netops: intent tenant-blue v2 compiled into 7 plans
netops: pre-flight validation passed, weights sum to 100
plan for host-a
  create  vxlan/blue-app  vni=100 local=10.0.0.1 group=239.1.1.1
  create  ovsdb/br-int    port=vxlan-blue-app type=vxlan
plan for br-int
  create
table=0,priority=200,ip,nw_dst=10.200.0.0/24,actions=output:vxlan-
blue-app
  remove  table=0,priority=100,ip,nw_dst=10.200.0.0/24,actions=drop
plan for checkout.blue.svc
  update  istio/VirtualService  v1=100 -> v1=90,v2=10
netops: wave 1 applied to host-a, overlay gate passed
netops: 7 plans, 5 changed, 2 converged, 0 failed, elapsed 18.4 s
```

In that run, seven plans across four dialects finished in eighteen seconds, and one intent file produced all of them. Our overlay gate proved the tunnel with real packets before the flow rules widened, so a broken underlay would have stopped the run rather than surfacing as an alert at breakfast. Nothing in the planner, the executor, or the rollout changed for this chapter. We added dialects and kept the discipline, which is what turns a network we can describe in one file into a network we can reason about.

Summary

Overall, we have placed four control dialects behind the planner without disturbing it at all. Our OVSDB client speaks JSON-RPC over the management socket and commits bridges, ports, and interfaces inside a single transaction, which finally gives us the atomicity a Linux host denied us. The netlink path creates VXLAN endpoints idempotently and reports an existing link as success rather than as a failure. Our flow tables then diff as sets, behind a normaliser which keeps the comparison stable between dumps.

Both Envoy and Istio joined us as data rather than as API ceremonies, with weight validation refusing a broken canary split before it reached the mesh. An intent file now sits above all four dialects, and several renderers compile it into ordinary plans which our existing waves, gates, and rollback handle unchanged. We deliberately left OpenFlow internals aside and orchestrated **`ovs-ofctl`** instead. In the next chapter, we turn the same discipline toward intrusion detection, where reading the wire replaces writing to it.

Chapter 7
Practical IDS/IPS Automation

Every chapter so far has changed something. This particular chapter reverses the direction, because a sensor only reads and yet the reading must never fall behind. A capture path which drops one packet in a thousand misses exactly the packet somebody will ask about a fortnight later. This chapter builds that path on libpcap, reconstructs flows, matches signatures with Vectorscan, and then hands the difficult judgement to Suricata and Zeek rather than reinventing what they already do well.

We will now assemble a capture ring which borrows buffers instead of copying them, a flow table keyed on the five-tuple, and a streaming scanner which survives a signature spanning two packets. Our rule management then becomes an ordinary change plan, alerts normalise into one shape before shipping, and nfqueue gives us an inline verdict whenever we choose to take one.

Reading Wire without Losing Packets

Capture Ring and Borrowed Buffer

Our opening chapter built **EthernetView** over a borrowed span and warned that a view outliving its buffer becomes a dangling reference. The chapter after it caught precisely that fault with AddressSanitizer. Both moments were preparation for this one, because a capture path is where borrowed memory earns its risk. We keep a ring of preallocated slots, hand a span into one slot to the parser, and recycle the slot only once the parser has finished with it. Our ring therefore arrives together with the capture loop which fills it, and that loop reaches for **pcap_next_ex** rather than **pcap_loop**, because a callback interface fights every attempt at structured shutdown.

In the following script, we will define the ring and drive it from a capture file:

```
class CaptureRing {
public:
    CaptureRing(std::size_t slots, std::size_t slot_bytes)
        : storage_(slots * slot_bytes), slot_bytes_(slot_bytes),
slots_(slots) {}

    std::span<std::byte> acquire() {
        const std::size_t i = head_ % slots_;
        ++head_;
        return std::span(storage_).subspan(i * slot_bytes_,
slot_bytes_);
    }

    std::size_t dropped() const { return dropped_; }
    void record_drop() { ++dropped_; }

private:
    std::vector<std::byte> storage_;
```

```
    std::size_t slot_bytes_;
    std::size_t slots_;
    std::size_t head_ = 0;
    std::size_t dropped_ = 0;
};

Result<void> capture(std::string_view source, CaptureRing& ring,
                     FlowTable& flows, std::stop_token stop) {
    char err[PCAP_ERRBUF_SIZE]{};
    pcap_t* h = pcap_open_offline(std::string(source).c_str(),
err);
    if (h == nullptr) {
        return fail(Category::transport, EIO, err);
    }
    const std::unique_ptr<pcap_t, decltype(&pcap_close)> guard(h,
pcap_close);

    pcap_pkthdr* hdr = nullptr;
    const u_char* data = nullptr;

    while (!stop.stop_requested()) {
        const int rc = pcap_next_ex(h, &hdr, &data);
        if (rc == -2) {
            break;
        }
        if (rc != 1) {
            ring.record_drop();
            continue;
        }
        auto slot = ring.acquire();
        std::memcpy(slot.data(), data,
                    std::min<std::size_t>(hdr->caplen,
slot.size()));
        flows.ingest(slot.first(hdr->caplen), hdr->ts);
    }
    return {};
}
```

One copy remains inside that loop, and its presence is deliberate rather than careless. The libpcap library owns the buffer it hands us and reuses it on the very next call, so a span into that memory expires immediately. Our slot copy costs a memcpy of at most fifteen hundred bytes and buys us a buffer whose lifetime we control completely. Everything downstream then borrows freely, and no parser ever needs to allocate.

Flow Reconstruction from Five-Tuple

A packet on its own tells us very little, since almost every interesting signature spans several of them. Our flow table therefore groups packets by the canonical five-tuple, keeps direction, and tracks the TCP state machine loosely. That word loosely is the operative one here, because a full reassembly implementation is a project rather than a section. We order the payload by sequence number and give up gracefully on anything pathological.

At this point, we will define the flow key and the table which accumulates payload:

```
struct FlowKey {
    std::uint32_t src_ip;
    std::uint32_t dst_ip;
    std::uint16_t src_port;
    std::uint16_t dst_port;
    std::uint8_t  proto;

    auto operator<=>(const FlowKey&) const = default;
};

FlowKey canonical(const FlowKey& k) {
    if (std::tie(k.src_ip, k.src_port) <= std::tie(k.dst_ip,
k.dst_port)) {
        return k;
    }
    return FlowKey{k.dst_ip, k.src_ip, k.dst_port, k.src_port,
k.proto};
}

class FlowTable {
public:
    void ingest(std::span<const std::byte> frame, timeval ts) {
        auto eth = as_ethernet(frame);
        if (!eth) {
            ++malformed_;
            return;
        }
        auto tuple = five_tuple(*eth);
        if (!tuple) {
            return;
        }

        Flow& f = flows_[canonical(*tuple)];
        f.last_seen = ts;
        f.bytes += frame.size();
        f.payload.append(payload_of(*eth));
        if (f.payload.size() > max_buffered_) {
            f.payload.erase(0, f.payload.size() - max_buffered_);
```

```
        }
    }

    std::flat_map<FlowKey, Flow>& flows() { return flows_; }

private:
    std::flat_map<FlowKey, Flow> flows_;
    std::size_t malformed_ = 0;
    static constexpr std::size_t max_buffered_ = 64 * 1024;
};
```

That sliding window over **`payload`** is the line which keeps us alive under load. A long-lived flow carrying a gigabyte would otherwise buffer all of it, and a few thousand such flows would exhaust memory within minutes.

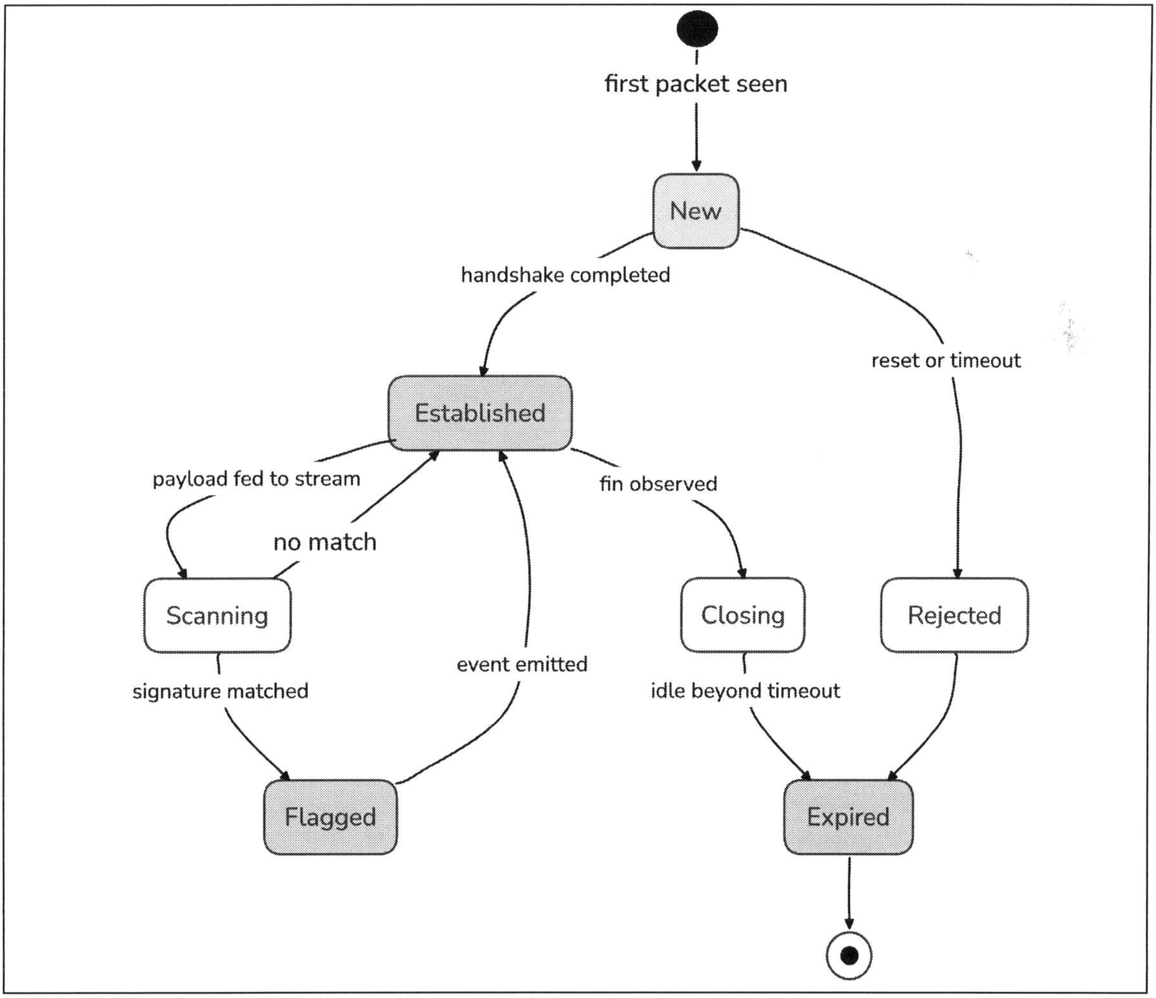

Sixty-four kilobytes covers every signature we care about while bounding our footprint predictably. Our earlier choice of **std::flat_map** also repays itself here, since a lookup happens for every packet and contiguous keys keep the cache warm.

Signature Matching with Vectorscan

Compiling Database Once

A regular expression runs one at a time in most code, and that arrangement collapses under a thousand signatures. The Vectorscan library compiles the whole set into one automaton and then matches all of them in a single pass. Our throughput therefore depends on the traffic rather than on how many patterns we loaded, which is exactly the property a sensor needs. The compilation costs perhaps two seconds for a large set, so we perform it once at startup and never again.

To begin, we start to compile a signature set and report precisely which pattern failed:

```
Result<Database> compile_signatures(std::span<const Signature>
sigs) {
    std::vector<const char*> exprs;
    std::vector<unsigned> flags;
    std::vector<unsigned> ids;

    for (const Signature& s : sigs) {
        exprs.push_back(s.pattern.c_str());
        flags.push_back(HS_FLAG_DOTALL | HS_FLAG_SINGLEMATCH |
                        (s.case_insensitive ? HS_FLAG_CASELESS :
0));
        ids.push_back(s.id);
    }

    hs_database_t* db = nullptr;
    hs_compile_error_t* err = nullptr;
    const hs_error_t rc = hs_compile_multi(
        exprs.data(), flags.data(), ids.data(),
        static_cast<unsigned>(exprs.size()),
        HS_MODE_STREAM, nullptr, &db, &err);

    if (rc != HS_SUCCESS) {
        const std::string detail = err ? err->message : "unknown
compile failure";
        const int which = err ? err->expression : -1;
        hs_free_compile_error(err);
        return fail(Category::validation, EINVAL,
                    std::format("signature at index {} rejected
```

```
({})",
                                              which, detail));
    }
    return Database(db);
}
```

Here, that **err->expression** field is worth handling properly rather than logging generically. The library names the index of the pattern which failed, so our message can identify the offending signature by its own number. A rule set of two thousand entries with one bad backreference is otherwise impossible to triage. We validate the entire set at startup and refuse to run with a partial database, since a silently dropped signature becomes a detection gap nobody notices.

Streaming Scans across Flow

A signature spanning two packets is the case which separates a real sensor from a demonstration. The library handles it through stream mode, where one stream holds automaton state for one flow across many scans. We open a stream when a flow appears, feed each payload segment as it arrives, and close the stream once the flow ends. A match then fires even when the pattern straddles a segment boundary.

We will now write the match callback and the per-flow feed:

```
static int on_match(unsigned id, unsigned long long, unsigned long
long to,
                    unsigned, void* ctx) {
    auto* hits = static_cast<std::vector<Hit>*>(ctx);
    hits->push_back(Hit{.signature_id = id, .offset = to});
    return 0;
}

Result<void> Scanner::feed(const FlowKey& key,
                           std::span<const std::byte> payload,
                           std::vector<Hit>& hits) {
    auto [it, fresh] = streams_.try_emplace(key, nullptr);
    if (fresh) {
        hs_stream_t* s = nullptr;
        if (hs_open_stream(db_.get(), 0, &s) != HS_SUCCESS) {
            streams_.erase(it);
            return fail(Category::internal, ENOMEM, "stream could
not be opened");
        }
        it->second.reset(s);
    }

    const hs_error_t rc = hs_scan_stream(
```

```
        it->second.get(), reinterpret_cast<const
char*>(payload.data()),
        static_cast<unsigned>(payload.size()), 0, scratch_.get(),
        on_match, &hits);

    if (rc != HS_SUCCESS && rc != HS_SCAN_TERMINATED) {
        return fail(Category::internal, EIO,
                    std::format("stream scan failed with {}",
                                static_cast<int>(rc)));
    }
    return {};
}
```

Once we run the scanner across a supplied capture, three hits surface from two flows.

```
netops: 1842 signatures compiled in 1.94 s
netops: scanning capture/lateral-movement.pcap
  hit sig=100411 flow=10.0.2.15:49722 -> 10.0.2.40:445 offset=2118
  hit sig=100411 flow=10.0.2.15:49722 -> 10.0.2.40:445 offset=6640
  hit sig=100518 flow=10.0.2.15:49730 -> 10.0.2.41:445 offset=1904
netops: 74210 packets, 3812 flows, 3 hits, 0 drops, elapsed 2.31 s
```

One scratch allocation appears in that call, and it must never be shared between threads. The library writes into scratch during a scan, so two threads sharing one allocation corrupt each other silently. Our scanner therefore keeps scratch for each thread and clones it at construction. Anybody profiling a multi-threaded sensor and finding impossible matches has almost certainly shared scratch by accident.

Suricata and Zeek as Managed Detectors

Rules as Change Plan

Our own scanner earns its place for custom patterns and for the parts of a pipeline we control. Both Suricata and Zeek nonetheless remain far better at the hard parts, namely protocol decoding, evasion handling, and a community rule set refreshed daily. We therefore manage them rather than replace them, and management is precisely what our planner already does. A rule file becomes a set of facts, and a rule change becomes an ordinary plan with a preview and a rollback.

In the following script, we will diff a wanted rule set against what is installed:

```
Result<ChangePlan> rule_plan(const RuleSet& wanted,
                             const std::filesystem::path& dir) {
    auto installed = load_rules(dir);
    if (!installed) {
```

```
        return std::unexpected(installed.error());
    }

    ChangePlan plan{.device = dir.string()};
    for (const Rule& r : wanted.rules) {
        const auto it = installed->find(r.sid);
        if (it == installed->end()) {
            plan.steps.push_back({.path = std::format("sid:{}",
r.sid),
                                  .desired = r.body, .action =
Action::create});
        } else if (it->second.body != r.body) {
            plan.steps.push_back({.path = std::format("sid:{}",
r.sid),
                                  .desired = r.body, .observed =
it->second.body,
                                  .action = Action::update});
        }
    }
    for (const auto& [sid, rule] : *installed) {
        if (!wanted.contains(sid) && wanted.manages(sid)) {
            plan.steps.push_back({.path = std::format("sid:{}",
sid),
                                  .observed = rule.body,
                                  .action = Action::remove});
        }
    }
    return plan;
}
```

In the output that follows, three steps appear, and the engine validates them before any reload happens.

```
plan for /etc/suricata/rules
  create  sid:1000021  alert tcp any any -> $HOME_NET 445
(msg:"lateral smb"; ...)
  update  sid:2027751  threshold changed from 5 to 20
  remove  sid:1000009  alert tcp any any -> any 23 (msg:"telnet";
...)
netops: 3 rule steps, suricata -T validation passed, reload
requested
```

That **`wanted.manages(sid)`** check prevents our worst possible mistake. A community rule set contributes tens of thousands of signatures which we did not write, and removing them because our own file lacks them would disable most of our detection. Our rule set therefore declares which identifier ranges it owns, and we only ever remove inside those ranges. We also run **suricata -T** before requesting a reload, since one syntax error stops the whole engine.

Consuming EVE and Zeek Events

The Suricata engine writes alerts as newline-delimited JSON into its EVE log, while Zeek publishes events through its Broker library. Both give us structured data without any linking against engine internals. Our consumer tails the EVE file, parses each line, and folds the result into our own event shape. A file tail sounds fragile until we handle rotation properly, which needs an inode check rather than a size check.

Let us now write the poll which survives a log rotation:

```
Result<void> EveReader::poll(std::vector<Event>& out) {
    struct stat st{};
    if (::stat(path_.c_str(), &st) == 0 && st.st_ino != inode_) {
        reopen();
    }

    std::string line;
    while (std::getline(stream_, line)) {
        const auto doc = nlohmann::json::parse(line, nullptr,
false);
        if (doc.is_discarded()) {
            ++malformed_;
            continue;
        }
        if (doc.value("event_type", "") != "alert") {
            continue;
        }
        out.push_back(Event{
            .source = "suricata",
            .severity =
severity_from(doc["alert"].value("severity", 3)),
            .signature = doc["alert"].value("signature",
"unnamed"),
            .sid = doc["alert"].value("signature_id", 0ULL),
            .src = doc.value("src_ip", ""),
            .dst = doc.value("dest_ip", ""),
            .at = doc.value("timestamp", "")});
    }
    stream_.clear();
    return {};
}
```

That **stream_.clear()** at the end is easy to omit and painful to diagnose. A stream which reached end of file sets its fail bit, and every later **getline** refuses to read even after fresh lines arrive. Our clear resets the state so the next poll continues from where we stopped. Anybody whose tailer works once and then falls permanently silent has met exactly the same problem.

Inline Blocking with 'nfqueue'

Verdict for Packets

We detect in order to tell somebody, and we prevent in order to stop the packet. The netfilter queue subsystem gives us the second option, since an iptables rule can hand a packet to userspace and wait for our verdict. Our process then accepts, drops, or marks each one in turn. Such power arrives with a matching responsibility, because a queue we stop reading becomes a network we have taken down.

So here, we will then write the verdict callback which evaluates and decides:

```
static int verdict(nfq_q_handle* q, nfgenmsg*, nfq_data* nfa, void*
ctx) {
    auto* engine = static_cast<Engine*>(ctx);
    nfqnl_msg_packet_hdr* ph = nfq_get_msg_packet_hdr(nfa);
    const std::uint32_t id = ph ? ntohl(ph->packet_id) : 0;

    unsigned char* data = nullptr;
    const int len = nfq_get_payload(nfa, &data);
    if (len <= 0) {
        return nfq_set_verdict(q, id, NF_ACCEPT, 0, nullptr);
    }

    const auto frame = std::span(reinterpret_cast<const
std::byte*>(data),
                                 static_cast<std::size_t>(len));
    const Decision d = engine->evaluate_within(frame,
std::chrono::microseconds(500));

    switch (d) {
    case Decision::block:
        engine->emit_block_event(frame);
        return nfq_set_verdict(q, id, NF_DROP, 0, nullptr);
    case Decision::allow:
    default:
        return nfq_set_verdict(q, id, NF_ACCEPT, 0, nullptr);
    }
}
```

We will now attach the queue and start the engine behind it:

```
sudo iptables -I FORWARD -p tcp --dport 445 \
    -j NFQUEUE --queue-num 0 --queue-bypass
sudo ./build/debug/netops ips --queue 0 --signatures
rules/custom.rules
```

As we run it, three packets are dropped, and the latency figures tell us whether we are safe to stay inline.

```
netops: attached to nfqueue 0, fail-open enabled via queue-bypass
netops: block 10.0.2.15:49722 -> 10.0.2.40:445 sig=100411 lateral
smb
netops: 41208 packets evaluated, 3 blocked, 0 queue overruns
netops: mean verdict latency 41 us, p99 210 us
```

That **`--queue-bypass`** flag is the most important detail in the whole command. With it present, traffic passes normally whenever our process is absent, so a crash degrades detection rather than connectivity. Without it, the same crash blackholes every packet matching the rule. We treat the flag as mandatory everywhere except a deliberate fail-closed deployment, and our tool refuses to attach without either the flag or an explicit override.

Fail-Open, Fail-Closed and Choice Between

Two postures exist, and neither one is universally right. A fail-open sensor keeps the network running when our process dies, which suits an enterprise where availability outranks containment. A fail-closed sensor stops the traffic instead, which suits a segment holding regulated data where a missed inspection is unacceptable. Our tool supports both and refuses to pick a default, since the choice belongs to whoever owns the consequence.

One safeguard applies to both postures. Our verdict path carries a deadline, and any evaluation exceeding it accepts the packet and records a timeout rather than blocking the queue. A regular expression which backtracks pathologically would otherwise stall the kernel queue and take the segment down with it. The library avoids catastrophic backtracking by design, and the deadline covers whatever else we might add later. Such a guard is never optional, because an inspection engine which can halt a network deserves a deadline more than it deserves another feature.

Alerts That Reach Somebody

Normalising to Event Shape

By this point, three detectors produce events, and each one describes the world differently. The Suricata output names a signature and a severity integer, Zeek names a notice and a kind, and our own scanner names an identifier and an offset. A downstream consumer should never have to learn all three vocabularies. Our normaliser therefore maps every source into one **`Event`** record with a fixed set of fields and one shared severity scale.

The severity mapping deserves particular care. Within Suricata, severity numbers from one as most urgent, while many downstream systems treat a higher number as worse, and a naive pass-through inverts the entire scale. Our mapping converts each source into a shared five-level enumeration with documented meanings. Anybody writing an alerting rule then reasons about our levels rather than about a vendor's integers.

Shipping to SIEM without Losing Events

A shipper which drops events during an outage is worse than no shipper at all, because it manufactures confident silence. Our shipper therefore spools to disk first and forwards from the spool, so a SIEM restart costs us latency rather than data. A batch keeps the connection efficient, while an fsync boundary keeps the spool honest. Nothing about this is novel, and skipping it is the most common reason an audit later finds a gap.

With that in place, we will implement the submit path which takes custody before forwarding:

```
Result<void> Shipper::submit(std::span<const Event> batch) {
    for (const Event& e : batch) {
        spool_ << to_json(e).dump() << '\n';
    }
    spool_.flush();
    if (::fdatasync(spool_fd_) != 0) {
        return fail(Category::internal, errno, "spool could not be
synced");
    }

    auto sent = forward(batch);
    if (!sent) {
        std::println("netops: siem unreachable, {} events held in
spool",
                     batch.size());
        return {};
    }
```

```
    return truncate_spool(batch.size());
}
```

Our success return when the SIEM is unreachable looks wrong and is entirely deliberate. The caller asked us to take custody of those events, and we did so, since the spool now holds them durably on disk. A failure returned here would stop the capture loop over a problem which resolves itself in a minute. We instead report the backlog, retry on a timer, and raise an alarm once the spool exceeds a threshold.

Enforcing mTLS as Control

Certificates as Facts

Now, mutual TLS is a control we can assert rather than merely hope for. The baseline from an earlier chapter already names facts about a host, and a certificate fits that model very neatly. We assert an issuer, a minimum key size, a remaining validity, and the presence of client authentication in the extended key usage. Each assertion becomes a probe, and a drifted certificate becomes an ordinary finding in the same report.

The expiry check deserves a threshold rather than a boolean. A certificate valid for another three days passes a naive check and then fails production on Thursday, so our fact declares a minimum remaining validity instead. That threshold of thirty days gives an operator room to act, and our drift report surfaces the finding long before anybody is woken. Such quiet prevention is the cheapest security work we ever do.

Detecting Unencrypted Traffic

A policy claiming that every internal service speaks mTLS is a claim we can verify on the wire. Our detector looks for a TLS record header at the start of each flow on a port we expect to be protected, and it raises a finding when those bytes look like anything else. Nothing about the check is sophisticated, and it catches the two failures which actually happen, namely a misconfigured sidecar and a service bypassing the mesh entirely.

Now we will write the header check and the sweep across guarded ports:

```
bool looks_like_tls(std::span<const std::byte> payload) {
    if (payload.size() < 6) {
        return false;
    }
    const auto b = [&](std::size_t i) { return
std::to_integer<int>(payload[i]); };
    const bool handshake = b(0) == 0x16;
    const bool version_ok = b(1) == 0x03 && b(2) <= 0x04;
    const bool client_hello = b(5) == 0x01;
```

```
    return handshake && version_ok && client_hello;
}

std::vector<Event> unprotected_flows(FlowTable& table,
                                     std::span<const std::uint16_t>
guarded) {
    std::vector<Event> out;
    for (auto& [key, flow] : table.flows()) {
        const bool watched = std::ranges::contains(guarded,
key.dst_port);
        if (!watched || flow.payload.empty()) {
            continue;
        }
        if (!looks_like_tls(as_bytes(flow.payload))) {
            out.push_back(Event{.source = "netops",
                                .severity = Severity::high,
                                .signature = "unencrypted traffic
on guarded port",
                                .src = to_string(key.src_ip),
                                .dst = to_string(key.dst_ip)});
        }
    }
    return out;
}
```

We can now run every detector across one day of captured mesh traffic:

```
./build/debug/netops ids \
    --pcap capture/mesh-day.pcap \
    --signatures rules/custom.rules \
    --guarded-ports 5432,6379,9092 \
    --siem https://siem.internal/api/events
```

All three detectors report through one shape, and the spool empties before we exit.

```
netops: 1842 signatures compiled, 3 detectors active
netops: 218441 packets, 9127 flows, 0 drops
  high    unencrypted traffic on guarded port  10.0.4.19 ->
10.0.4.60:5432
  high    lateral smb                          10.0.2.15 ->
10.0.2.40:445
  medium  suricata ET SCAN nmap                10.0.9.7  ->
10.0.2.0/24
netops: 3 events normalised, 3 shipped, spool empty, elapsed 6.82 s
```

That first finding is the one worth quiet celebration. A Postgres connection reaching port 5432 without a TLS handshake means some service is bypassing the mesh completely, and no configuration audit would ever have found it. Our capture path saw the truth rather than the intention. We report it at high severity and let somebody decide, exactly as we did with an open compliance finding in an earlier chapter. A control we verify on the wire is a control, and everything else is a diagram.

Summary

We have now built a sensor which reads without falling behind. Our capture ring copies once from libpcap and then lends spans downstream, which finally makes the borrowed-buffer discipline from our opening chapter pay for itself. The flow table groups packets by a canonical five-tuple and bounds its own memory through a sliding window. Our scanner then matches nearly two thousand signatures in one pass through Vectorscan, with stream mode catching patterns which straddle a packet boundary.

Our two managed engines stayed exactly where they belong, since ordinary change plans never remove a rule outside the ranges we own. The nfqueue path gave us an inline verdict behind a deadline and a mandatory bypass flag, our shipper spools to disk before forwarding so an outage costs latency rather than data, and an mTLS check verified on the wire what a policy had only promised. In the next chapter, we carry the same habits into cloud networking, where an API replaces the wire.

Chapter 8
Cloud Network Automation

Our sensor read packets from a wire, and this chapter reads and writes an API instead. A cloud removes the wire, the SSH session, and the candidate datastore all at once, replacing them with HTTP calls which succeed before their effect exists. That final property is the one which catches everybody at least once. A subnet creation returns an identifier while the resource is still settling, so code written for a switch behaves badly against a cloud.

We will now provision a VPC through the AWS SDK for C++, reach Azure over its REST interface because no C++ management SDK covers networking, and place both behind one provider interface. The load balancers and private endpoints then become declarative sets, throttling meets a backoff with jitter, and a cost estimate appears before any apply.

Changes after API Replacing Wire

Eventual Consistency and Waiter Pattern

A NETCONF commit either applied or it did not, and the reply told us which. A cloud API grants us no such courtesy. A call creating a subnet returns success and an identifier while the control plane still propagates that change across its own systems, so an immediate follow-up referencing the identifier may fail with a not-found error. Nothing is broken when that happens, and a blind retry is the wrong response.

The waiter pattern handles the situation properly. We poll the resource until it reports the state we expect, with a bounded number of attempts and a deadline beyond which we treat matters as a genuine failure. Every mature cloud toolkit ships waiters for exactly this reason. Our own wrapper adds one thing they often lack, namely a failure message naming both the resource and the state it never reached.

Our next step is to trace one create through its settling period:

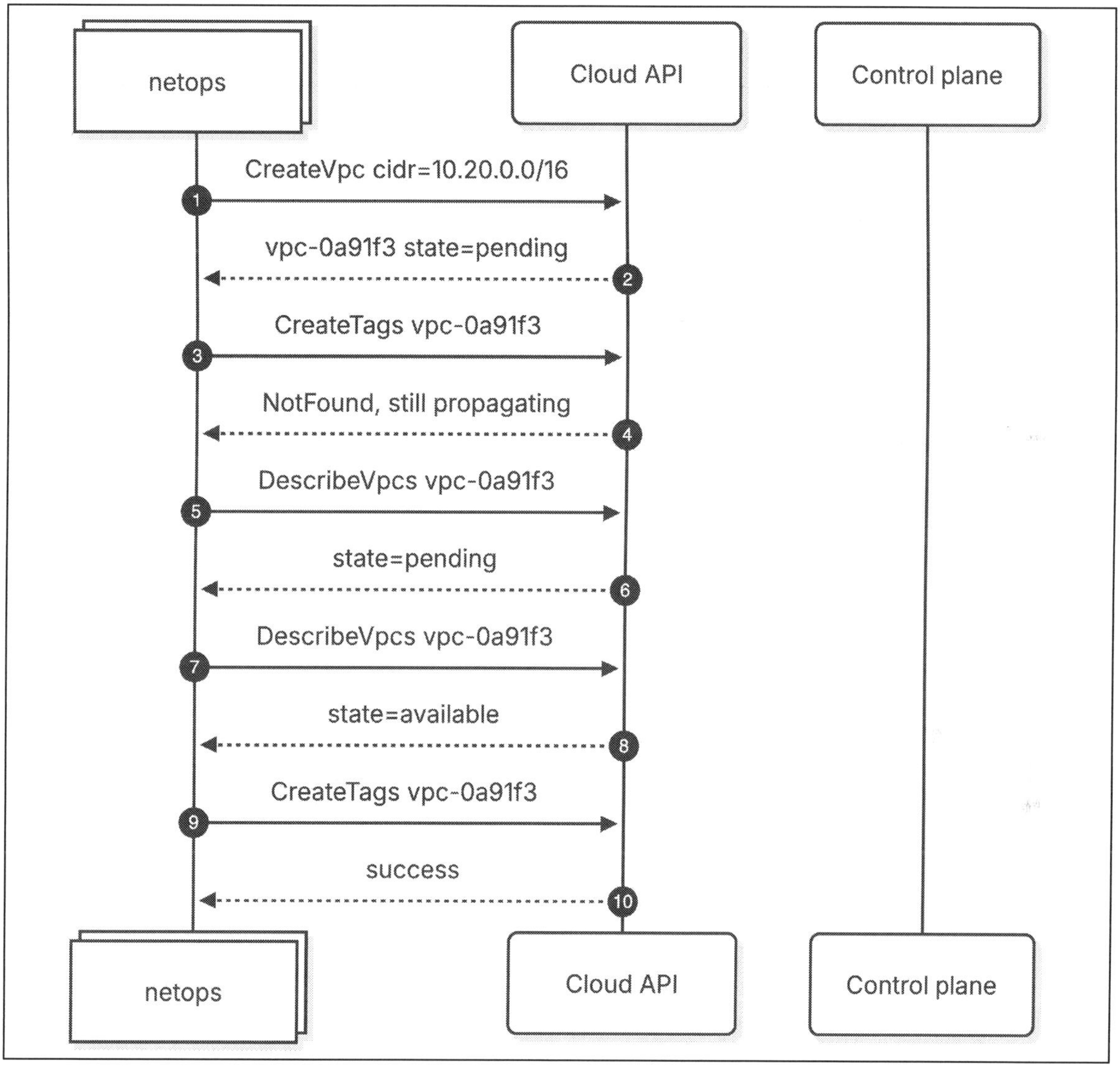

Idempotency through Tags and Client Tokens

Our earlier idempotency came from reading a path and comparing a value. Such resources break that habit, because a create call has no natural identity to compare against. A second **`CreateVpc`** produces a second VPC with a different identifier and identical configuration, which is the most expensive kind of mistake we can make. We therefore give every resource an owner tag and a logical name, and we look for that pair before creating anything at all.

A client request token closes the remaining window. A token supplied with a create call makes the operation idempotent for a period, so a retry after a timeout returns the original resource rather than a duplicate. We derive the token deterministically from our logical name and the plan version, which means a rerun of the same plan reuses the same token. Such determinism turns a network timeout from a duplication risk into an ordinary retry.

Provisioning VPC with AWS SDK

Building Essential Components

The AWS SDK for C++ builds every service by default, which produces roughly four hundred libraries and an hour of compilation. Nobody needs that for network automation. We therefore build only the components our tool actually touches, namely EC2 for VPC work, ELBv2 for load balancers, and CloudWatch for metrics. The compilation then finishes in a few minutes, and our container image stays a reasonable size.

We will now request those three components and nothing further:

```
set(AWS_COMPONENTS ec2 elasticloadbalancingv2 monitoring)
find_package(AWSSDK REQUIRED COMPONENTS ${AWS_COMPONENTS})

target_link_libraries(libnetops PRIVATE ${AWSSDK_LINK_LIBRARIES})
target_compile_definitions(libnetops PRIVATE USE_IMPORT_EXPORT)
```

One configuration detail makes every exercise in this chapter free. The SDK accepts an endpoint override, so pointing it at LocalStack exercises the same code paths without touching a real account. Our tool reads that override from configuration rather than from a compile-time flag, which means one binary runs against a laboratory and against production alike. Anybody testing cloud automation against a live account is paying for confidence they could have had for nothing.

To make that concrete, we will start LocalStack and point our tool at it:

```
docker run -d --name localstack -p 4566:4566 \
    -e SERVICES=ec2,elbv2,cloudwatch localstack/localstack:latest

export NETOPS_AWS_ENDPOINT=http://localhost:4566
```

As shown below, LocalStack reports which services came up, and our tool confirms the override before it issues a single call.

```
localstack: Ready.
localstack: ec2, elbv2, cloudwatch available on 4566

netops: aws endpoint override http://localhost:4566
netops: region eu-west-1, credentials from environment
netops: ec2 DescribeVpcs returned 1 vpc
```

Nothing in our source differs between a laboratory run and a production run, and only that environment variable changes. Our SDK calls, our retry wrapper, and our tagging all behave identically against LocalStack, which is what makes every exercise in this chapter free to repeat as often as we like. Anybody wanting to point at a real account clears the override and supplies credentials in the usual way.

Subnets, Route Tables and Plan

A VPC on its own carries no traffic, since the subnets and route tables decide everything which matters. Our plan therefore covers all three together, and the ordering between them is not optional. A subnet needs its VPC, a route needs its gateway, and an association needs both of those. We express such relations as an ordered plan rather than as a dependency graph, because a linear order is far easier to preview and to reverse.

In the following script, we will create a VPC idempotently and wait until it settles:

```
Result<std::string> AwsProvider::ensure_vpc(const VpcSpec& spec) {
    if (auto found = find_by_tag("netops:name", spec.name); found)
{
        return *found;
    }

    Aws::EC2::Model::CreateVpcRequest req;
    req.SetCidrBlock(spec.cidr);
    req.SetClientToken(token_for(spec.name, spec.plan_version));

    auto out = ec2_.CreateVpc(req);
    if (!out.IsSuccess()) {
        return fail(Category::protocol,

static_cast<int>(out.GetError().GetErrorType()),
                    out.GetError().GetMessage());
    }

    const std::string id = out.GetResult().GetVpc().GetVpcId();
    if (auto tagged = with_retry([&] { return tag(id, spec.name);
}); !tagged) {
        return std::unexpected(tagged.error());
    }

    return wait_until(std::chrono::seconds(60), [&] {
        return vpc_state(id) == "available";
    }).transform([id] { return id; });
}
```

On a first run, four resources appear, and the summary reports what was skipped.

```
netops: vpc plan for tenant-blue (endpoint http://localhost:4566)
  create  vpc/tenant-blue             cidr=10.20.0.0/16
  create  subnet/tenant-blue-a        cidr=10.20.1.0/24 az=us-east-1a
  create  subnet/tenant-blue-b        cidr=10.20.2.0/24 az=us-east-1b
  create  route-table/tenant-blue     0.0.0.0/0 -> igw-tenant-blue
netops: vpc-0a91f3 available after 1.8 s
netops: 4 resources created, 0 duplicated, elapsed 6.4 s
```

That **`0 duplicated`** figure is not decoration. Our tool reports how many creates were skipped because a tagged resource already existed, which turns idempotency into something visible rather than assumed. A second run of the same plan reports four skips and zero creates, so anybody watching learns immediately whether the tagging works. We hold that line strictly, since a duplicated VPC gets discovered by finance rather than by monitoring.

REST Everywhere

Azure Resource Manager over Boost.Beast

We are better served by honesty than by optimism here. The Azure SDK for C++ covers storage, identity, and core plumbing, and it does not cover network resource management at all. Anybody expecting parity with the Python or Go libraries will be disappointed quickly. We therefore reach Azure Resource Manager over its REST interface, which is thoroughly documented and entirely workable from Boost.Beast. The authentication step is the only genuinely fiddly part, since we acquire a bearer token from the identity endpoint using a service principal, cache it until shortly before expiry, and attach it to every request. Our **`Secret`** type from an earlier chapter holds the client secret, so the value never reaches a log or a core dump.

From here, we will create a virtual network through a declarative PUT:

```
Result<std::string> AzureProvider::ensure_vnet(const VnetSpec&
spec) {
    auto token = token_.acquire();
    if (!token) {
        return std::unexpected(token.error());
    }

    const auto path = std::format(

"/subscriptions/{}/resourceGroups/{}/providers/Microsoft.Network"
        "/virtualNetworks/{}?api-version=2024-05-01",
        subscription_, spec.resource_group, spec.name);

    nlohmann::json body{
```

```
        {"location", spec.location},
        {"tags", {{"netops:name", spec.name}}},
        {"properties", {{"addressSpace",
            {{"addressPrefixes",
nlohmann::json::array({spec.cidr})}}}}}}};

    auto res = put_json(path, body, *token);
    if (!res) {
        return std::unexpected(res.error());
    }

    if (res->at("properties").value("provisioningState", "") !=
"Succeeded") {
        return wait_until(std::chrono::seconds(120), [&] {
            auto now = get_json(path, *token);
            return now && now->at("properties")
                                  .value("provisioningState", "") ==
"Succeeded";
        }).transform([&] { return res->value("id", ""); });
    }
    return res->value("id", "");
}
```

A PUT against Azure Resource Manager is declarative by design, which suits us rather better than the create-and-check dance AWS requires. The same document sent twice produces the same resource instead of a second one, so our idempotency arrives free from the protocol itself. Our tag still travels along regardless, because a report which cannot name the owner of a resource is a report nobody acts upon.

Single Cloud Interface and Several Backends

Two providers now exist, and a third will eventually arrive. Our interface therefore names outcomes rather than services, with methods for a network, a subnet, a route, a load balancer, and a private endpoint. Each provider translates those into whatever its own API calls them. The previous chapter kept three detectors behind one event shape, and this is the same instinct applied to provisioning.

We will now declare the interface and the factory which resolves a provider by name:

```
class CloudProvider {
public:
    virtual ~CloudProvider() = default;
    virtual std::string_view name() const = 0;

    virtual Result<std::string> ensure_network(const NetworkSpec&)
```

```
= 0;
    virtual Result<std::string> ensure_subnet(const SubnetSpec&) =
0;
    virtual Result<void>        ensure_route(const RouteSpec&) = 0;
    virtual Result<std::string> ensure_balancer(const
BalancerSpec&) = 0;
    virtual Result<std::string> ensure_endpoint(const
EndpointSpec&) = 0;

    virtual Result<ChangePlan>  plan(const CloudIntent&) = 0;
};

Result<std::unique_ptr<CloudProvider>>
provider_for(std::string_view kind,
                                                   const Config&
cfg) {
    if (kind == "aws") {
        return std::make_unique<AwsProvider>(cfg);
    }
    if (kind == "azure") {
        return std::make_unique<AzureProvider>(cfg);
    }
    return fail(Category::validation, EINVAL,
                std::format("no provider registered for '{}'",
kind));
}
```

Our interface deliberately omits anything a single cloud invented. The transit gateways, Private Link service aliases, and peering quirks all live inside a provider rather than in the shared vocabulary. Such restraint keeps the abstraction honest, because an interface stretched to cover every feature stops abstracting anything at all. Whenever a provider needs something unique, our intent file names it under a provider block and the shared path ignores it.

We will now picture how one intent reaches two clouds:

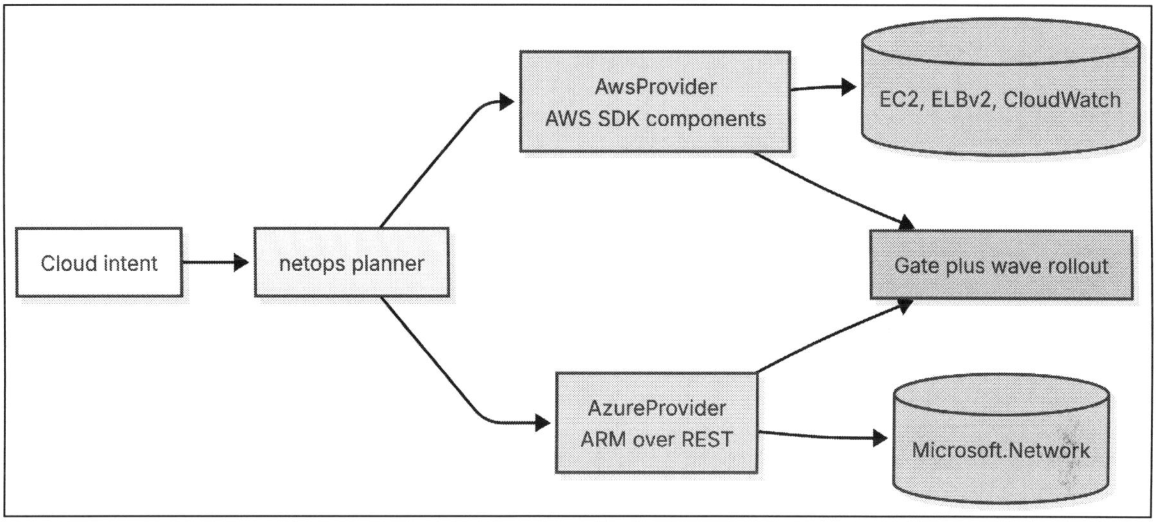

Load Balancers and Private Endpoints

Target Groups as Declarative Set

A load balancer is mostly a set of targets, and sets diff cleanly as we learned with flow tables. Our tool reads the registered targets, computes the set we want, and then registers or deregisters only the difference. Nothing gets replaced wholesale, because deregistering everything and re-registering it drops live connections for no reason whatsoever. The health check settings then travel as ordinary leaves inside the very same plan.

In the following script, we will diff the registered targets against the wanted set:

```
Result<ChangePlan> AwsProvider::balancer_plan(const BalancerSpec&
spec) {
    auto current = registered_targets(spec.target_group_arn);
    if (!current) {
        return std::unexpected(current.error());
    }

    ChangePlan plan{.device = spec.name};
    const auto have =
std::ranges::to<std::set<std::string>>(*current);

    for (const std::string& want : spec.targets) {
        if (!have.contains(want)) {
            plan.steps.push_back({.path = std::format("target/{}",
want),
                                  .desired = "registered",
```

```
                                        .action = Action::create});
        }
    }
    for (const std::string& existing : have) {
        if (!std::ranges::contains(spec.targets, existing)) {
            plan.steps.push_back({.path = std::format("target/{}",
existing),
                                  .observed = "registered",
                                  .action = Action::remove});
        }
    }

    if (would_empty(plan, have) && !spec.allow_drain) {
        return fail(Category::validation, EINVAL,
                    std::format("plan would empty target group {}",
spec.name));
    }
    return plan;
}
```

That guard protects us from an obvious disaster. Our planner refuses any plan which would leave a target group empty, unless somebody passes an explicit drain flag. A configuration mistake removing every target otherwise takes a service offline while every individual API call reports success. We learned the same lesson with rule identifiers in the previous chapter, and the shape of the protection is identical here.

Private Endpoints over Public Paths

A managed database reachable across the public internet is a finding rather than an architecture. A private endpoint solves it by placing the service inside our own address space, so traffic never leaves the provider network. Our tool creates them declaratively and then proves the result by resolving the service name from inside a subnet. We verify because a created endpoint with a missing DNS zone association looks perfectly healthy and still resolves publicly.

Two checks make that verification meaningful. We resolve the service hostname from inside the VPC and require a private address within our own CIDR, and we then attempt a connection from a subnet holding no route to the internet. Both together prove the private path genuinely carries traffic. A single check on the endpoint status proves only that the control plane created something.

Throttling, Retries and Cost

Backoff with Jitter

Every cloud API throttles, and a fleet-scale plan will meet those limits regularly. A naive retry loop makes the situation worse, since every client backs off by the same interval and then retries in unison. Our backoff therefore multiplies the delay and adds randomness, which spreads the retries apart in time. Nothing here is novel, and its absence is the most common reason a cloud automation run collapses at scale.

Accordingly, we will wrap any operation in a retry which respects both jitter and a ceiling:

```
template <typename Fn>
auto with_retry(Fn&& op, int attempts = 6) -> decltype(op()) {
    static thread_local std::mt19937 rng{std::random_device{}()};
    std::chrono::milliseconds delay{200};

    for (int i = 1; i <= attempts; ++i) {
        auto out = op();
        if (out || !is_throttling(out.error())) {
            return out;
        }
        if (i == attempts) {
            return out;
        }
        std::uniform_int_distribution<int> jitter(0,
delay.count());
        std::this_thread::sleep_for(delay +
std::chrono::milliseconds(jitter(rng)));
        delay = std::min(delay * 2,
std::chrono::milliseconds{8000});
    }
    return op();
}
```

That **`is_throttling`** predicate carries the whole design. We retry a rate limit and a temporary service failure, and we never retry a validation error or a permission denial. A malformed request retried six times wastes eight seconds and teaches us nothing, while a retried permission failure hides a genuine misconfiguration behind noise. Our predicate therefore lists the retryable conditions explicitly rather than treating every failure as transient.

Costs of Plan

A cloud plan differs from a device plan in one uncomfortable way, since applying it spends money.

A NAT gateway costs a fixed amount for every hour it exists, a load balancer costs more, and cross-zone traffic costs more again. Our preview therefore names the recurring charge of every resource it would create, using a static price table rather than a live pricing API. An approximate figure shown early beats an exact figure discovered later.

We will now preview a tenant plan with costing enabled:

```
./build/debug/netops cloud plan \
    --intent lab/tenant-blue-cloud.yaml --provider aws --with-cost
```

Each resource carries its own charge, and the summary totals them honestly.

```
plan for aws/tenant-blue
  create  vpc/tenant-blue             no recurring charge
  create  subnet/tenant-blue-a        no recurring charge
  create  nat-gateway/tenant-blue     32.40 USD per month plus data
  create  balancer/checkout-nlb       16.20 USD per month plus LCU
  create  endpoint/rds-blue            7.30 USD per month
netops: 5 resources, estimated 55.90 USD per month, data transfer
excluded
netops: dry run, nothing applied
```

That figure of fifty-six dollars a month sounds trivial until the same template runs in forty accounts. Our estimate has caught more mistakes at review than any technical check, because a reviewer who sees a NAT gateway they did not expect asks the obvious question immediately. We label the figure as approximate and exclude data transfer deliberately, since a promise of precision we cannot keep would be worse than a rough number honestly marked.

Cloud Telemetry into Collector

Pulling Metrics on Budget

Our cloud metrics arrive by request rather than by stream, and every request carries a charge. A collector polling two hundred metrics every ten seconds becomes a visible line on a bill, which is a failure mode our earlier gNMI work never had. Our collector therefore batches metric queries into one call, widens the interval for anything not driving a decision, and caches results aggressively between waves.

To make that concrete, we will implement a batched collection behind the retry wrapper:

```
Result<std::vector<Sample>> CloudWatchCollector::collect(
        std::span<const MetricRef> refs,
        std::chrono::system_clock::time_point since) {
    Aws::CloudWatch::Model::GetMetricDataRequest req;
```

```
    req.SetStartTime(Aws::Utils::DateTime(to_time_t(since)));
    req.SetEndTime(Aws::Utils::DateTime(
        to_time_t(std::chrono::system_clock::now())));

    int id = 0;
    for (const MetricRef& r : refs) {
        Aws::CloudWatch::Model::MetricDataQuery q;
        q.SetId(std::format("m{}", id++));
        q.SetMetricStat(stat_for(r));
        q.SetReturnData(true);
        req.AddMetricDataQueries(std::move(q));
    }

    return with_retry([&] () -> Result<std::vector<Sample>> {
        auto out = cw_.GetMetricData(req);
        if (!out.IsSuccess()) {
            return fail(Category::protocol, 0,
out.GetError().GetMessage());
        }
        return to_samples(out.GetResult().GetMetricDataResults());
    });
}
```

One call carrying five hundred queries costs the same as one call carrying a single query. Our batching therefore reduces the charge by nearly three orders of magnitude against a request for each metric, and the code is barely any longer. We also request the widest period which still serves the decision, since a five-minute period costs less than a one-minute period and a capacity trend needs neither.

Gate for Cloud Changes

Our gate interface has already served switches, servers, and overlays, and cloud resources fit it without any modification. What changes is the evidence we agree to accept. A balancer gate waits for healthy targets rather than for an interface state, a route gate resolves a name and connects, and an endpoint gate proves a private address. Each one reuses the wave rollout exactly as the earlier chapters did.

We can now apply the whole tenant intent behind the balancer gate:

```
./build/debug/netops cloud apply \
    --intent lab/tenant-blue-cloud.yaml --provider aws \
    --gate balancer --apply
```

Every stage reports, and the gate names each target as it becomes healthy.

```
netops: intent tenant-blue-cloud v1 compiled into 5 plans
netops: estimated 55.90 USD per month, approved by --apply
netops: wave 1 applied to vpc/tenant-blue, 4 resources available
netops: gate waiting on target group checkout-nlb
netops:   i-0a4f21 healthy, i-0b7c88 healthy, 0 unhealthy
netops: gate passed after 42 s
netops: 5 plans, 5 changed, 0 converged, 0 failed, elapsed 71.4 s
```

Those forty-two seconds of gate waiting are entirely normal for a load balancer, because health checks need several successful probes before a target is treated as healthy. Our earlier settling delays were arbitrary, whereas this one derives from the health check configuration itself. We read the interval and the threshold, multiply them, and add a small margin. Such derivation removes a magic number from our code and replaces it with the truth, which is how a cloud change we can price, preview, and prove becomes a cloud change somebody can approve.

Summary

We have now taught our tool to work where the wire disappears entirely. In a cloud, eventual consistency forced a waiter around every create, while tags and deterministic client tokens replaced the path comparison which gave us idempotency everywhere else. The AWS SDK arrived as three components rather than four hundred, and LocalStack made every exercise free to run. Then Azure joined over REST, since no C++ management SDK covers its networking, and a declarative PUT gave us idempotency for nothing.

One provider interface then absorbed both clouds while keeping vendor peculiarities inside the providers themselves. The target groups diffed as sets behind a guard which refuses to empty one, private endpoints were proven by resolving from inside a subnet, and throttling met a backoff with jitter and an explicit retryable list. Our preview now prices a plan before anybody approves it. In the next chapter, we turn toward Kubernetes as the control plane for AI clusters.

CHAPTER 9

KUBERNETES AS AI CLUSTER CONTROL PLANE

Our cloud work provisioned networks around virtual machines, and an AI cluster moves the interesting part inside a scheduler. A pod arrives, a scheduler places it, and a chain of plugins decides which interfaces and which accelerators it receives. Nothing in that chain resembles a switch or a subnet, and yet a surprising share of the failures look exactly like networking failures. This chapter puts our tool in charge of the parts we can genuinely assert.

We will now reach the API server over REST with a service-account token, use server-side apply as our commit, and watch rather than poll for readiness. The reachability block from our intent file then gains one more renderer, producing network policies alongside the flow rules it already produced. After that, Multus gives a pod a second interface, device plugins expose accelerators as resources, and we finish with a pod bound to an RDMA-capable device.

Why Cluster Became Network?

Single Pod Network Not Enough

A default pod network carries control traffic perfectly well and suits ordinary services completely. An AI workload breaks that assumption on its first distributed training run. The gradient exchange between eight nodes saturates whatever the primary interface offers, while the same interface still carries health probes, log shipping, and the API server conversation. Once we mix the two, a checkpoint upload can starve a collective operation, which surfaces as a training slowdown nobody can explain.

Two interfaces solve the problem cleanly. A primary network keeps the ordinary cluster traffic, while a secondary network carries collective traffic across dedicated hardware. Our work lies in making that second attachment reproducible rather than artisanal, since a cluster where three nodes were configured by hand fails in ways nobody enjoys diagnosing. Here, Multus provides the mechanism, and our tool provides the discipline around it. One consequence deserves stating early, because a pod with two interfaces has two routing tables, two MTUs, and two failure modes, so our verification must check both rather than assuming symmetry between them. An MTU mismatch on the secondary network is the most common fault we will meet in this territory. In the next chapter, we show why that particular mismatch destroys RDMA throughput rather than merely reducing it.

Kind Cluster and Service Account

Everything in this chapter runs against kind, which builds a cluster from containers in under two minutes. Our exercises therefore cost nothing and reset cleanly, which matters a lot when a network policy mistake isolates a workload. We disable nothing unnecessarily, label one worker as though it carried accelerators, and mount the host modules so a software RDMA device can appear. Such labelling lets us exercise scheduling logic without owning a single GPU.

We will now define the cluster our exercises assume:

```yaml
kind: Cluster
apiVersion: kind.x-k8s.io/v1alpha4
name: netops-ai

networking:
  podSubnet: "10.244.0.0/16"

nodes:
  - role: control-plane
  - role: worker
    labels:
      netops.io/accelerator: "simulated"
      netops.io/rdma-capable: "true"
    extraMounts:
      - hostPath: /lib/modules
        containerPath: /lib/modules
        readOnly: true
  - role: worker
    labels:
      netops.io/accelerator: "none"
```

The authentication step comes next, and a service account is the least painful path available. We create an account, bind a role granting exactly the verbs our tool needs, and read the projected token from inside a pod or from a secret outside it. Our tool never parses a kubeconfig, since exec plugins and credential helpers turn that into a project of its own. A token and a CA bundle cover everything we require.

Talking to API Server

Applying Server-Side

No official Kubernetes client exists for C++, and the situation is far less troubling than it sounds. The API server speaks ordinary REST with JSON bodies, and Boost.Beast already carries our HTTP work from two earlier chapters. What we gain by working directly is an understanding of the API rather than of a binding. What we lose is generated types, and a handful of small structs covers everything this chapter needs. Above that transport sits the server-side apply mechanism, which is what makes our commit declarative. A PATCH carrying the **`application/apply-patch+yaml`** content type hands the API server a desired shape, and the server merges it while tracking which fields we own. Our tool therefore stops caring whether a resource already exists, exactly as the declarative PUT let us stop caring in the previous chapter.

In the following script, we will build a client from a service-account token and a cluster CA:

```
class KubeClient {
public:
    static Result<KubeClient> from_service_account(
            const std::string& host,
            const std::filesystem::path& token_path,
            const std::filesystem::path& ca_path) {
        auto token = read_file(token_path);
        if (!token) {
            return std::unexpected(token.error());
        }

        boost::asio::ssl::context
tls(boost::asio::ssl::context::tlsv13_client);
        boost::system::error_code ec;
        tls.load_verify_file(ca_path.string(), ec);
        if (ec) {
            return fail(Category::validation, ec.value(),
                        std::format("cluster CA unreadable ({})",
ec.message()));
        }
        tls.set_verify_mode(boost::asio::ssl::verify_peer);

        return KubeClient(host, Secret(std::move(*token)),
std::move(tls));
    }

    Result<nlohmann::json> apply(std::string_view path,
                                 const nlohmann::json& manifest);
    Result<nlohmann::json> get(std::string_view path);

private:
    std::string host_;
    Secret token_;
    boost::asio::ssl::context tls_;
};
```

In the following script, we will implement that apply behind our existing retry wrapper:

```
Result<nlohmann::json> KubeClient::apply(std::string_view path,
                                         const nlohmann::json&
manifest) {
    const auto target =
std::format("{}?fieldManager=netops&force=true", path);

    boost::beast::http::request<boost::beast::http::string_body>
```

```
req{
        boost::beast::http::verb::patch, target, 11};
    req.set(boost::beast::http::field::host, host_);
    req.set(boost::beast::http::field::authorization,
            std::format("Bearer {}", token_.expose()));
    req.set(boost::beast::http::field::content_type,
            "application/apply-patch+yaml");
    req.body() = manifest.dump();
    req.prepare_payload();

    return with_retry([&]() -> Result<nlohmann::json> {
        auto res = send(req);
        if (!res) {
            return std::unexpected(res.error());
        }
        if (res->result_int() >= 400) {
            return fail(Category::protocol, res->result_int(), res-
>body());
        }
        return nlohmann::json::parse(res->body(), nullptr, false);
    });
}
```

That **fieldManager** parameter is the detail which prevents a fight nobody wins. Two controllers applying the same resource without distinct managers overwrite each other endlessly, and the resulting flapping is genuinely hard to diagnose. Our manager name identifies every field our tool owns, so anybody editing an unrelated field keeps their change. We pass **force=true** deliberately, because a conflict on a field we already own should resolve in our favour.

Watching Polling

A pod becoming ready is an event rather than a state we should interrogate repeatedly. The watch API streams changes as newline-delimited JSON over one long-lived connection, which suits our gates precisely. We open a watch with a resource version, consume events until our condition holds, and reconnect on the disconnections which arrive as a matter of routine. We could poll the same information every second, and we would also hammer the API server across a large cluster.

We then proceed to implement a watch which resumes cleanly after a disconnect:

```
Result<void> KubeClient::watch_until(
        std::string_view path,
        std::chrono::seconds deadline,
        const std::function<bool(const nlohmann::json&)>&
satisfied) {
    const auto until = std::chrono::steady_clock::now() + deadline;
```

```
    std::string version = "0";

    while (std::chrono::steady_clock::now() < until) {
        auto stream =
open_watch(std::format("{}&watch=1&resourceVersion={}",
                                                path, version));
        if (!stream) {
            return std::unexpected(stream.error());
        }

        std::string line;
        while (stream->next_line(line)) {
            const auto ev = nlohmann::json::parse(line, nullptr,
false);
            if (ev.is_discarded()) {
                continue;
            }
            version =
ev["object"]["metadata"].value("resourceVersion", version);
            if (satisfied(ev["object"])) {
                return {};
            }
        }
    }
    return fail(Category::timeout, ETIMEDOUT,
                std::format("watch on {} expired after {} s",
                            path, deadline.count()));
}
```

Below, three resources apply, and the watch reports each transition as it arrives.

```
netops: applied NetworkAttachmentDefinition/ai-secondary
(fieldManager=netops)
netops: applied NetworkPolicy/blue-app-egress
netops: watching pod/trainer-0 for condition Ready
netops:   ContainerCreating, 2 network attachments pending
netops:   PodScheduled=True node=netops-ai-worker
netops:   Ready=True after 11.4 s
netops: 3 resources applied, 1 watch satisfied
```

That **resourceVersion** handling deserves attention, since a watch disconnects routinely rather than exceptionally. A reconnect from the version we last saw resumes the stream without replaying old events or missing new ones. A reconnect from zero instead floods us with the current state of every object, which on a large cluster arrives as several megabytes. Our loop therefore tracks the version on every event rather than only at the start.

We will now trace the apply and the watch as one sequence:

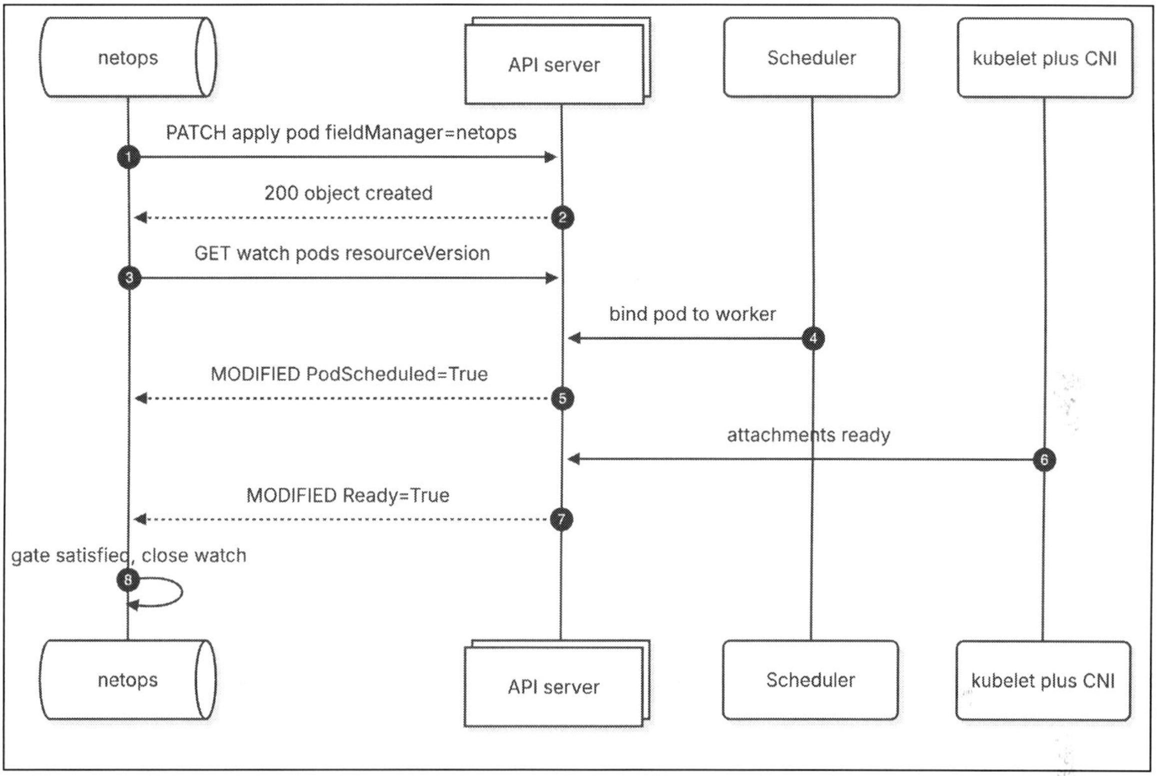

Network Policy and Reachability

Renderer for Same Intent

Our intent file already carries a reachability block, and an earlier chapter turned it into flow rules for a virtual switch. That very same block now produces network policies for a cluster, because the statement of intent was never about a mechanism. A renderer translates each rule into a **`NetworkPolicy`** naming pod selectors, ports, and a direction. Nothing in the intent file changes, and nothing in the planner learns which target it happens to serve.

With that in place, we will render one reachability rule into a policy document:

```
Result<nlohmann::json> render_policy(const ReachabilityRule& rule,
                                     std::string_view ns) {
    nlohmann::json ports = nlohmann::json::array();
    for (std::uint16_t p : rule.ports) {
        ports.push_back({{"protocol", "TCP"}, {"port", p}});
    }
```

```
    nlohmann::json peers = nlohmann::json::array();
    if (rule.to != "any") {
        peers.push_back({{"podSelector",
            {{"matchLabels", {{"netops.io/segment", rule.to}}}}}});
    }

    const bool permit = rule.action == Reach::allow;

    return nlohmann::json{
        {"apiVersion", "networking.k8s.io/v1"},
        {"kind", "NetworkPolicy"},
        {"metadata", {{"name", std::format("{}-egress",
rule.from)},
                      {"namespace", ns}}},
        {"spec", {
            {"podSelector", {{"matchLabels",
                {{"netops.io/segment", rule.from}}}}},
            {"policyTypes", nlohmann::json::array({"Egress"})},
            // An empty egress array denies all egress for the
selected pods.
            {"egress", permit
                ? nlohmann::json::array({{{"to", peers}, {"ports",
ports}}})
                : nlohmann::json::array()}}}};
}
```

A deny rule renders as an empty egress list rather than as an explicit denial, which surprises everybody exactly once. The Kubernetes policy model permits by default and denies only whatever no rule allows, so an empty list attached to a selector blocks all egress from those pods. Our renderer therefore expresses a deny by producing a policy which permits nothing at all. We document that inversion in the code, since a reviewer meeting an empty array otherwise assumes a bug.

Verifying Policy with Traffic

A network policy applied is not a network policy enforced, because a CNI plugin without policy support silently ignores every one of them. Such silence is the worst possible failure, since the manifests look correct while the traffic flows freely. We therefore verify with traffic in both directions, proving that a permitted path works and a denied path genuinely fails. Both halves matter equally, and most teams check only the first.

So here, we will then test one permitted path and one denied path from inside the workload:

```
kubectl -n blue exec deploy/blue-app -- \
    timeout 3 nc -z blue-db 5432 && echo "allowed path ok"
```

```
kubectl -n blue exec deploy/blue-app -- \
    timeout 3 nc -z 1.1.1.1 443 || echo "denied path blocked"
```

Both directions confirm, and our gate records the evidence rather than the intention.

```
allowed path ok
denied path blocked
netops: policy gate for segment blue-app
netops:   allow blue-app -> blue-db:5432   verified
netops:   deny  blue-app -> any            verified
netops: policy gate passed
```

Our negative test carries a timeout for a very specific reason. A blocked connection under most policy implementations hangs rather than refusing, so a test without a deadline waits forever and reports nothing useful. Roughly three seconds distinguishes a blocked path from a slow one reliably enough. We fold both checks into a **Gate** implementation, which means a policy change travels through the same wave rollout as every other change in this book.

Secondary Networks with Multus

macvlan Attachment

The Multus plugin attaches additional interfaces by reading an annotation on a pod and consulting a **NetworkAttachmentDefinition**. That definition names a CNI plugin and its configuration, which is precisely where hardware requirements usually creep in. A macvlan attachment needs no special hardware at all, so every exercise here runs on a laptop while exercising the same machinery an SR-IOV attachment uses. Only the plugin name and the resource request differ afterwards.

We will now define the secondary network our training pods will attach to:

```
apiVersion: k8s.cni.cncf.io/v1
kind: NetworkAttachmentDefinition
metadata:
  name: ai-secondary
  namespace: blue
spec:
  config: |
    {
      "cniVersion": "1.0.0",
      "type": "macvlan",
      "master": "eth0",
      "mode": "bridge",
      "mtu": 9000,
```

```
    "ipam": {
      "type": "host-local",
      "subnet": "10.30.0.0/16",
      "rangeStart": "10.30.1.10",
      "rangeEnd": "10.30.1.200"
    }
  }
```

That MTU of nine thousand is the field which matters most on this page. A secondary network carrying collective traffic wants jumbo frames, and every hop between the endpoints must agree on the value. Our tool asserts it as a fact on the attachment definition and again on the interface inside a running pod, because the two disagree far more often than anybody expects. An MTU declared here yet unsupported by the underlay produces silent loss under load.

SR-IOV and Data

A real accelerator fabric uses SR-IOV virtual functions rather than macvlan, and a laptop cannot provide one. We would waste the time of anybody following along by pretending otherwise. Our companion repository therefore supplies a captured description of a genuine SR-IOV node, including the device plugin configuration, the advertised resources, and the allocation a pod received. Our exercise then writes the validator against that data.

Such an arrangement teaches rather more than it first appears to. Anybody can read a manifest, whereas writing a validator which spots a virtual function shortage, a mismatched driver, or a resource name typo requires understanding the whole allocation model. Our validator runs against the supplied data during the unit suite, so it stays honest without any hardware present.

Scheduling onto Right Silicon

Device Plugins and Extended Resources

A device plugin advertises hardware to the scheduler as an extended resource with a vendor-prefixed name. An accelerator appears as **nvidia.com/gpu**, an RDMA device as **rdma/rdma_shared_device_a**, and a virtual function as whatever a vendor chose. Our tool reads the capacity and allocatable figures for those names, which tells us how much hardware exists and how much remains free. Nothing more sophisticated is needed to prevent the commonest scheduling failure.

In the following script, we will read accelerator capacity across every node:

```
Result<std::vector<NodeCapacity>> KubeClient::accelerator_capacity(
        std::string_view resource) {
    auto doc = get("/api/v1/nodes");
    if (!doc) {
```

```
        return std::unexpected(doc.error());
    }

    std::vector<NodeCapacity> out;
    for (const auto& node : doc->at("items")) {
        const auto& status = node.at("status");
        const auto total =
status["capacity"].value(std::string(resource), "0");
        const auto free =
status["allocatable"].value(std::string(resource), "0");
        if (total == "0") {
            continue;
        }
        out.push_back(NodeCapacity{
            .node = node["metadata"].value("name", ""),
            .resource = std::string(resource),
            .total = std::stoul(total),
            .allocatable = std::stoul(free),
            .numa_node = numa_hint(node)});
    }
    return out;
}
```

One simulated node and two supplied ones report together, with the free figures beside the totals.

```
netops: resource rdma/rdma_shared_device_a
  node                          total  allocatable  numa
  netops-ai-worker                  4            4     0
  gpu-node-07 (supplied)            8            2     0
  gpu-node-08 (supplied)            8            8     1
netops: 20 devices present, 14 allocatable across 3 nodes
```

That allocatable column is where a pending pod gets explained. A cluster with plenty of total capacity and almost nothing allocatable leaves pods pending indefinitely, and the scheduler event says only that no node matched. Our report shows the shortage before anybody submits the workload. We also refuse a plan requesting more devices than remain free, which converts a silently pending pod into a clear rejection at plan time.

Topology Awareness and NUMA Alignment

An accelerator and its network interface should sit on the same NUMA node, and the difference is far from marginal. A misaligned pair forces every transfer across the processor interconnect, which costs bandwidth and adds latency to precisely the operations we care about most. Fortunately, Kubernetes handles the alignment through its topology manager, provided we request resources in a way which lets the manager succeed at all.

Two conditions must both hold. The kubelet needs a topology manager policy of **`single-numa-node`** or **`restricted`**, and our pod must request its accelerator and its network device inside the same container rather than across two. A split across containers defeats the manager entirely, since alignment gets computed for each container separately. Our validator checks both conditions and refuses a pod specification which cannot possibly align.

We can now picture the whole path from our tool to a placed pod:

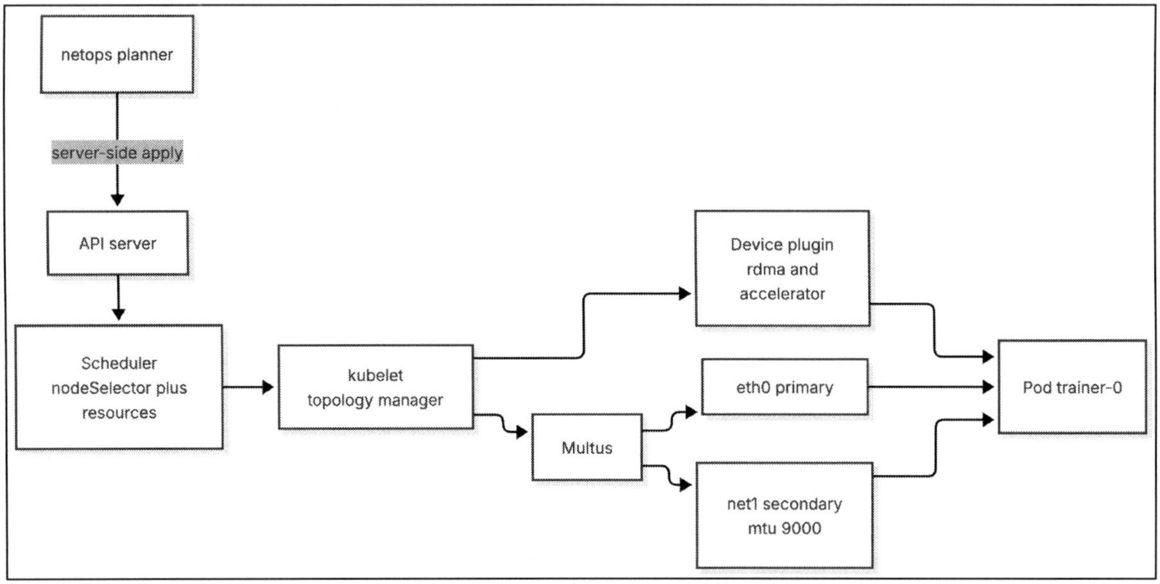

Pod Bound to RDMA NIC

Assembling Pod Spec

Everything in this chapter now converges on one manifest. A pod requests an accelerator and an RDMA device in the same container, carries a Multus annotation naming the secondary attachment, and lands on a node labelled as fabric-capable. Our tool generates that specification from intent rather than accepting it by hand, because three of those four elements are easy to omit and each omission fails in a different way.

Now we will generate the pod which the next chapter builds upon:

```
apiVersion: v1
kind: Pod
metadata:
  name: trainer-0
  namespace: blue
  labels:
    netops.io/segment: blue-app
```

```
  annotations:
    k8s.v1.cni.cncf.io/networks: ai-secondary
spec:
  nodeSelector:
    netops.io/rdma-capable: "true"
  containers:
    - name: trainer
      image: netops-dev:latest
      command: ["sleep", "infinity"]
      resources:
        limits:
          rdma/rdma_shared_device_a: 1
          netops.io/simulated-accelerator: 1
      securityContext:
        capabilities:
          add: ["IPC_LOCK"]
```

That **IPC_LOCK** capability is the one people forget most reliably. The RDMA path requires pinned memory registration, and the pinning fails without that capability regardless of how correct everything else appears. A container which starts happily and then fails inside the verbs library is almost always missing it. Our generator adds the capability whenever a pod requests an RDMA resource, and our validator rejects any specification where one appears without the other.

Proving Binding

A pod which reached Ready has proven very little about its fabric. We therefore verify from inside the container, checking that the secondary interface exists at the declared MTU and that an RDMA device is visible to the verbs library. Both checks read rather than write, so they cost nothing and can run on every single deployment. Our gate then accepts or rejects the wave on that evidence rather than on a status field.

We will now read the three facts which decide whether this pod can carry collective traffic:

```
kubectl -n blue exec trainer-0 -- ip -o link show net1
kubectl -n blue exec trainer-0 -- ibv_devinfo -l
kubectl -n blue exec trainer-0 -- sh -c 'ulimit -l'
```

All three confirm, and our gate summarises them in the form a report can carry.

```
2: net1@if12 mtu 9000 state UP mode DEFAULT
1 HCA found:
    rxe0
unlimited
netops: fabric gate for pod/trainer-0
netops:   secondary interface net1 present, mtu 9000 as declared
```

```
netops:   rdma device rxe0 visible to verbs
netops:   memory locking unlimited, IPC_LOCK effective
netops: fabric gate passed, pod ready for collective traffic
```

All three facts arrive together there, and a pod missing any one of them fails later rather than sooner. Our secondary interface carries the MTU we declared, a verbs-capable device is visible inside the container, and memory locking is unlimited. The device named **rxe0** is SoftRoCE rather than hardware, which is exactly what lets this exercise run on an ordinary laptop. In the next chapter, we begin from this pod and put that device to work. A cluster which can tell us where its silicon sits is a cluster we can schedule honestly.

Summary

We have now placed a Kubernetes cluster behind the same planner which already handles switches, servers, and clouds. Our client reaches the API server over REST with a service-account token, and server-side apply gave us a declarative commit behind a field manager which prevents controller fights. A watch replaced polling, with the resource version tracked on every event so a routine disconnect resumes rather than replays several megabytes.

The reachability block from our intent file gained one more renderer, producing network policies which we verified with traffic in both directions rather than by reading manifests. Then, Multus attached a second interface through macvlan at nine thousand bytes, device plugins exposed accelerators as schedulable resources, and our validator refused any pod which could not align across NUMA. One pod now holds a secondary interface, a visible verbs device, and unlimited memory locking. In the next chapter, we put that device to work.

CHAPTER 10
RDMA AND GPU FABRIC AUTOMATION

Our pod from the previous chapter holds a verbs device, a second interface at nine thousand bytes, and unlimited memory locking. Everything it needs in order to move data now exists, and nothing yet proves the fabric underneath will carry that data well. An AI fabric fails differently from every network we have automated so far, because it degrades quietly rather than breaking loudly. A training run simply takes eleven hours instead of six.

We will now bring up SoftRoCE, enumerate devices and ports from C++, and assert lossless behaviour as a baseline rather than as folklore. Our validators run against captured output from a genuine fabric supplied in the repository, so we write the checks without owning the hardware. After that, link statistics reveal pause storms and flapping ports, a topology parser explains what a collective library decided, and a fabric gate proves the path with real traffic.

Versatility of AI Fabric

Lossless Ethernet

An ordinary TCP connection treats a dropped packet as information, since congestion control depends on that loss signal. The RDMA transport treats the same drop as a catastrophe, because it expects delivery in order and recovers slowly whenever ordering breaks. A single lost packet inside a collective operation can stall every participant, which turns one hardware hiccup into a cluster-wide pause. Our fabric therefore has to avoid loss rather than recover from it gracefully.

Two mechanisms cooperate to achieve that. The priority flow control pauses a traffic class at the link level when a buffer fills, while explicit congestion notification marks packets so a sender slows before any buffer overflows. Both must be configured consistently on every port along a path, and such consistency is exactly what fails in practice. One switch carrying the wrong priority mapping turns a lossless fabric into a lossy one for whichever flows traverse it. A further failure mode deserves naming immediately, because priority flow control applied too aggressively spreads congestion backwards through a fabric, a behaviour usually called a pause storm, and a storm can idle an entire rail. Such an outcome is considerably worse than the loss it prevented. Our validators therefore check both the presence of the configuration and the statistics which reveal that configuration misbehaving.

Rails, Fat Trees, and Traffic

A general-purpose datacenter fabric optimises for any-to-any traffic between unpredictable endpoints. An AI cluster does the opposite, since its traffic pattern is known in advance and repeats on every iteration. The gradient exchange happens between the same ranks, in the same order, at the same moments. Such predictability lets us build a rail-optimised topology, where each accelerator holds its own dedicated path to its peers on other nodes.

The arrangement matters for automation rather than merely for design. A rail-optimised fabric means the eighth accelerator on every node shares one switch, so a single failed leaf degrades one rail across the whole cluster instead of isolating one node. Our monitoring must therefore group by rail rather than by node, or a serious fault appears as eight unrelated minor ones. We label every port with its rail during discovery for exactly that reason.

From here, we will picture one rail across four nodes:

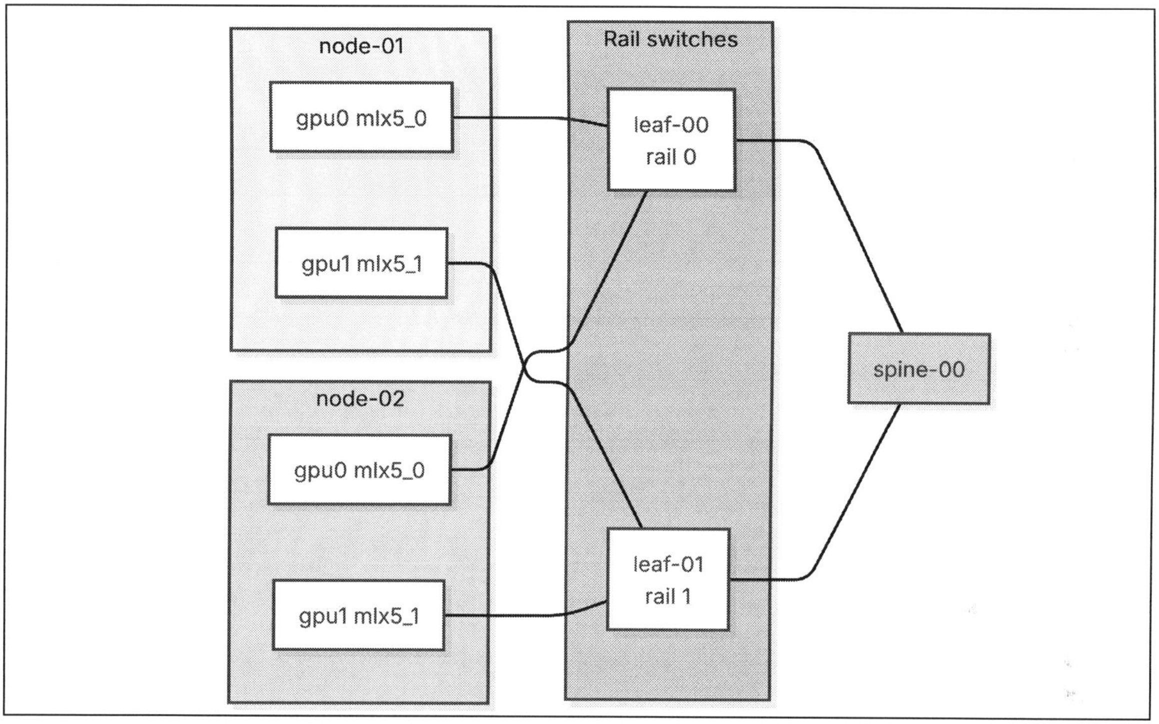

SoftRoCE and Device Discovery

RXE on Host

The kernel provides a software RoCE implementation named rxe, which presents a verbs device over any ordinary Ethernet interface. The performance is irrelevant here, since we are automating configuration and health rather than measuring throughput. What matters is that every query, every validator, and every path test in this chapter runs identically against rxe and against real hardware. Our code never learns which one it received.

We will now create a software RDMA device over the existing interface:

```
sudo modprobe rdma_rxe
sudo rdma link add rxe0 type rxe netdev eth0
rdma link show
```

One caveat belongs beside that convenience. A software device reports a link layer of Ethernet and a port MTU derived from the underlying interface, so an MTU assertion behaves realistically against it. What rxe cannot reproduce is congestion behaviour, since no hardware buffer exists to fill and no pause frame is ever generated. Our PFC and ECN work therefore runs against supplied data from a real fabric, exactly as the SR-IOV material did in the previous chapter.

Querying Devices and Ports

Our earlier decision to stay away from verbs programming holds firmly here. We open no queue pairs, register no memory, and post no work requests, because all three belong to an application rather than to an automation tool. What we do instead is query, which the same library exposes through a handful of calls. A device list, a device attribute structure, and a port attribute structure tell us everything a health check needs.

In the following script, we will enumerate every device and every port it carries:

```
Result<std::vector<FabricPort>> discover_ports() {
    int n = 0;
    ibv_device** list = ibv_get_device_list(&n);
    if (list == nullptr) {
        return fail(Category::internal, errno, "no rdma devices
enumerated");
    }
    const std::unique_ptr<ibv_device*,
decltype(&ibv_free_device_list)> guard(
        list, ibv_free_device_list);

    std::vector<FabricPort> out;
    for (int i = 0; i < n; ++i) {
        ibv_context* ctx = ibv_open_device(list[i]);
        if (ctx == nullptr) {
            continue;
        }

        ibv_device_attr dev{};
        if (ibv_query_device(ctx, &dev) == 0) {
            for (std::uint8_t p = 1; p <= dev.phys_port_cnt; ++p) {
                ibv_port_attr port{};
                if (ibv_query_port(ctx, p, &port) != 0) {
                    continue;
                }
                out.push_back(FabricPort{
                    .device = ibv_get_device_name(list[i]),
                    .port = p,
                    .state = to_string(port.state),
                    .link_layer = port.link_layer ==
IBV_LINK_LAYER_ETHERNET
                                        ? "Ethernet" : "InfiniBand",
```

```
                    .active_mtu = mtu_bytes(port.active_mtu),
                    .rate_gbps = rate_of(port)});
            }
        }
        ibv_close_device(ctx);
    }
    return out;
}
```

Our software device appears beside three supplied hardware ports, and one of them is down.

```
netops: rdma discovery on trainer-0
  device    port  state   link       active mtu  rate
  rxe0         1  ACTIVE  Ethernet         4096  10 Gb/s
  mlx5_0       1  ACTIVE  Ethernet         4096  400 Gb/s
(supplied)
  mlx5_1       1  ACTIVE  Ethernet         4096  400 Gb/s
(supplied)
  mlx5_2       1  DOWN    Ethernet            0  0 Gb/s
(supplied)
netops: 4 ports across 3 devices, 1 down, elapsed 0.04 s
```

That active MTU of 4096 is worth pausing over, because it is not the interface MTU we set to nine thousand. The RDMA layer negotiates its own path MTU from a fixed set of values, and 4096 is the largest which fits inside a nine thousand byte frame once headers are accounted for. An interface left at 1500 bytes forces the negotiation down to 1024 instead, which costs roughly a third of achievable throughput. Our validator therefore asserts the RDMA MTU rather than the interface MTU.

Validating PFC and ECN across Fabric

Baseline for Lossless Behaviour

Our baseline mechanism from an earlier chapter asserted packages and services, and a fabric baseline asserts in exactly the same way. We name the priority carrying RDMA traffic, the flow control state for that priority, the congestion marking thresholds, and the DSCP value which maps traffic into the class. Each assertion becomes a fact, and any mismatch becomes a finding inside an ordinary report.

With that in place, we will write the baseline which describes a lossless rail:

```
name: roce-fabric-baseline
version: 4
```

```yaml
facts:
  - kind: rdma_priority
    priority: 3
    dscp: 26
  - kind: pfc
    priority: 3
    state: enabled
    applies_to: all_fabric_ports
  - kind: ecn
    algorithm: dcqcn
    min_threshold_kb: 150
    max_threshold_kb: 1500
    probability_percent: 1
  - kind: rdma_mtu
    bytes: 4096
  - kind: trust_mode
    mode: dscp
```

That **`trust_mode`** fact catches a failure which wastes whole afternoons. A switch trusting layer two priority rather than DSCP ignores the marking our hosts apply, so traffic lands in the default class and receives no lossless treatment whatsoever. Everything else appears configured correctly, and the fabric quietly discards packets under load. We assert the trust mode explicitly, because no symptom ever points at it.

Validator against Captured Fabric Data

Nobody following along owns a rail of four hundred gigabit switches, and we will not pretend otherwise. Our repository supplies captured configuration and statistics from a real RoCEv2 fabric of thirty-two ports, including two deliberate misconfigurations. The exercise here is writing the validator rather than owning the fabric, and the validator is the part which transfers straight into production. Anybody with hardware points the same binary at their own devices.

Once this is in place, we will compare every captured port against the baseline:

```cpp
std::vector<Finding> validate_lossless(const FabricBaseline& base,
                                       std::span<const PortConfig>
ports) {
    std::vector<Finding> out;

    for (const PortConfig& p : ports) {
        if (!p.pfc_enabled.contains(base.rdma_priority)) {
            out.push_back({.host = p.switch_name, .port = p.name,
                           .fact = "pfc",
                           .wanted = std::format("priority {}
enabled",
```

```
base.rdma_priority),
                              .observed = join(p.pfc_enabled, ","),
                              .severity = Severity::high});
        }
        if (p.trust_mode != base.trust_mode) {
            out.push_back({.host = p.switch_name, .port = p.name,
                              .fact = "trust_mode",
                              .wanted = base.trust_mode,
                              .observed = p.trust_mode,
                              .severity = Severity::high});
        }
        if (p.ecn_min_kb != base.ecn_min_kb || p.ecn_max_kb !=
base.ecn_max_kb) {
            out.push_back({.host = p.switch_name, .port = p.name,
                              .fact = "ecn",
                              .wanted = std::format("{}..{} kb",
                                                     base.ecn_min_kb,
base.ecn_max_kb),
                              .observed = std::format("{}..{} kb",
                                                     p.ecn_min_kb,
p.ecn_max_kb),
                              .severity = Severity::medium});
        }
    }
    return out;
}
```

We will now run that validator against the supplied capture:

```
./build/debug/netops fabric validate \
    --baseline lab/roce-fabric-baseline.yaml \
    --data data/fabric-rail3-captured.json
```

The validation below surfaces three findings, and the final line names the consequence rather than the symptom.

```
validation against roce-fabric-baseline v4
switch      port        fact        wanted              observed
leaf-07     Ethernet12  pfc         priority 3 enabled  priority 0
enabled
leaf-07     Ethernet12  trust_mode  dscp                cos
spine-02    Ethernet31  ecn         150..1500 kb        150..3000
kb
netops: 32 ports checked, 29 compliant, 2 high, 1 medium
```

```
netops: rail 3 holds one non-lossless path, leaf-07 Ethernet12
```

One port out of thirty-two is enough to ruin a rail, and our report says so plainly. Any traffic crossing **leaf-07 Ethernet12** receives no lossless treatment, while every other path behaves correctly, so the symptom appears as intermittent slowness for whichever ranks happen to traverse it. Our earlier compliance habit of naming the consequence rather than only the finding matters more here than anywhere else in this book.

Link Health, Pause Storms and Flaps

Reading Error Statistics

Every fabric port maintains statistics, and misreading them is rather easier than reading them. A pause frame tally which grows steadily indicates a healthy congestion response, whereas one which grows in bursts of millions indicates a storm. An absolute figure therefore tells us almost nothing, while a rate across a known interval tells us a considerable amount. Our reader takes two samples and reports the difference over the elapsed time. Nothing else gives a usable signal, because a port which has been up for ninety days accumulates enormous totals from an incident last March. We sample every ten seconds, keep a short history, and discard anything older than the window we care about.

In the following script, we will read the statistics and convert two samples into rates:

```
Result<LinkStats> read_link_stats(std::string_view iface) {
    const auto base = std::format("/sys/class/net/{}/statistics",
iface);
    LinkStats s;
    s.rx_pause    = read_u64(std::format("{}/rx_pause_frames",
base)).value_or(0);
    s.tx_pause    = read_u64(std::format("{}/tx_pause_frames",
base)).value_or(0);
    s.rx_errors   = read_u64(std::format("{}/rx_errors",
base)).value_or(0);
    s.rx_dropped = read_u64(std::format("{}/rx_dropped",
base)).value_or(0);
    s.carrier_changes = read_u64(
        std::format("/sys/class/net/{}/carrier_changes",
iface)).value_or(0);
    s.at = std::chrono::steady_clock::now();
    return s;
}

LinkRates rates_between(const LinkStats& a, const LinkStats& b) {
    const double secs = std::max(
```

```
        0.001, std::chrono::duration<double>(b.at - a.at).count());
    return LinkRates{
        .pause_per_sec   = (b.rx_pause - a.rx_pause) / secs,
        .errors_per_sec  = (b.rx_errors - a.rx_errors) / secs,
        .dropped_per_sec = (b.rx_dropped - a.rx_dropped) / secs,
        .flaps           = b.carrier_changes - a.carrier_changes};
}
```

That **`carrier_changes`** value is the most useful single figure on a fabric port. A link which transitions twice has been reconfigured, whereas a link which transitions forty times in an hour is failing and will fail worse. Our threshold sits deliberately low, since a flapping fabric port costs far more than a maintenance visit. We treat any repeated transition as a finding rather than as noise.

Detecting Flapping Link

A flapping link damages an AI workload considerably more than a failed one. A dead port removes itself from every path, and the fabric routes around it within seconds. A flapping port keeps rejoining instead, so collective operations repeatedly rebuild their communication plan while every rank waits on the slowest path. Such behaviour reaches a training log as random slowdowns rather than as a network fault.

We are now ready to detect a flap inside a sliding window:

```
class FlapDetector {
public:
    FlapDetector(std::chrono::minutes window, unsigned threshold)
        : window_(window), threshold_(threshold) {}

    std::vector<Finding> observe(std::string_view iface, const
LinkStats& now) {
        auto& hist = history_[std::string(iface)];
        hist.push_back(now);

        const auto cutoff = now.at - window_;
        std::erase_if(hist, [&](const LinkStats& s) { return s.at <
cutoff; });

        if (hist.size() < 2) {
            return {};
        }
        const auto flaps =
            hist.back().carrier_changes -
hist.front().carrier_changes;
        if (flaps < threshold_) {
            return {};
        }
```

```
        return {Finding{.host = std::string(iface),
                        .fact = "carrier_changes",
                        .wanted = std::format("< {} per {} min",
                                              threshold_,
window_.count()),
                        .observed = std::format("{}", flaps),
                        .severity = Severity::high}};
    }

private:
    std::chrono::minutes window_;
    unsigned threshold_;
    std::flat_map<std::string, std::vector<LinkStats>> history_;
};
```

A sweep across three ports finds two faults which no status check would have reported.

```
netops: fabric health sweep, 10 s sampling, 15 min window
  port           pause/s   errors/s   drops/s   flaps
  mlx5_0/eth2       12.4        0.0       0.0       0
  mlx5_1/eth3    18420.0        0.0    1180.2       0
  mlx5_2/eth4        0.0        0.0       0.0      23
netops: high  pause storm on mlx5_1/eth3, 18420 pause frames per
second
netops: high  flapping link mlx5_2/eth4, 23 carrier changes in 15
min
netops: 2 findings, rail 1 and rail 2 degraded
```

Both findings describe faults which a status check would have missed entirely. Our second port reports up, active, and correctly configured while pausing eighteen thousand times a second, which starves everything sharing its traffic class. The third port reports up as well, between twenty-three disappearances. We report both at high severity and name the affected rail, because a cluster team fixes a rail rather than a port.

Collective Traffic and Topology Awareness

NCCL Library

A collective library chooses its own communication plan at startup, and that choice determines which links carry the load. The NCCL library inspects the topology, builds rings and trees across the available devices, and prints its decision whenever asked. We do not influence that plan directly, and we very much want to know what it decided. A plan crossing the processor interconnect instead of a rail explains a slow job immediately. Our parser therefore reads the topology dump and extracts the rings, the channel widths, and the transport chosen for each hop.

Anything falling back to shared memory or to sockets where RDMA was expected becomes a finding, and such a fallback is the most common cause of a training run which turns inexplicably slower after a maintenance window.

Accordingly, we will check a captured plan for transports which should never appear:

```
Result<std::vector<Finding>> check_nccl_plan(const
std::filesystem::path& dump) {
    auto lines = read_lines(dump);
    if (!lines) {
        return std::unexpected(lines.error());
    }

    std::vector<Finding> out;
    for (std::string_view line : *lines) {
        if (line.contains("via NET/Socket") || line.contains("via
SHM")) {
            out.push_back({.host = host_in(line),
                           .fact = "nccl_transport",
                           .wanted = "NET/IB or NET/EFA",
                           .observed =
std::string(transport_in(line)),
                           .severity = Severity::high});
        }
        if (line.contains("NCCL_IB_DISABLE=1")) {
            out.push_back({.host = host_in(line),
                           .fact = "nccl_ib",
                           .wanted = "enabled",
                           .observed = "disabled by environment",
                           .severity = Severity::high});
        }
    }
    return out;
}
```

That environment check exists because somebody always sets the variable during a debugging session and then forgets it. A cluster carrying **NCCL_IB_DISABLE=1** in a job template runs correctly and slowly forever. Our check reads the plan rather than the template, so the finding appears regardless of where the setting originally came from.

GPUDirect, EFA, and TPU

A further three technologies deserve placing accurately, and none of them is something we will program here. The first, GPUDirect RDMA, lets a network device read accelerator memory without a host bounce, which removes a copy from every transfer. Our tool verifies its presence by reading the module state and the device capability rather than by exercising it. A missing GPUDirect path shows up as roughly halved bandwidth, and the remedy is a driver rather than our code.

The Elastic Fabric Adapter on AWS reaches a similar goal through a different interface, namely libfabric rather than verbs. Our discovery therefore checks for either provider and records which one it found. The Google accelerators present the sharpest contrast, since a TPU pod exposes no host-visible fabric device at all and its interconnect stays entirely under provider management. Nothing in this chapter applies there, and saying so plainly serves better than a strained analogy.

Fabric Gate for AI Workloads

Proving Path with 'rping'

A validated configuration and healthy statistics still leave one question open, namely whether the path carries RDMA traffic at all. The **rping** utility establishes a genuine connection between two endpoints, which proves the whole stack from verbs down to the wire. Our gate runs it between the pod from the previous chapter and a peer, then treats any failure as blocking. Nothing simpler gives us the same assurance.

We will now prove the path between two pods on the same rail:

```
kubectl -n blue exec trainer-1 -- rping -s -a 10.30.1.11 -C 5 &
kubectl -n blue exec trainer-0 -- rping -c -a 10.30.1.11 -C 5 -v
```

In the output below, five exchanges complete, and our gate reports all four of its conditions.

```
ping data: rdma-ping-0:
ABCDEFGHIJKLMNOPQRSTUVWXYZ[\]^_`abcdefghijklmnopqr
ping data: rdma-ping-1:
BCDEFGHIJKLMNOPQRSTUVWXYZ[\]^_`abcdefghijklmnopqrs
netops: fabric gate for rail 0
netops:   rping trainer-0 -> trainer-1 completed 5 exchanges
netops:   rdma mtu 4096 on both endpoints
netops:   pause rate 12.4/s, within threshold
netops:   0 carrier changes in window
netops: fabric gate passed
```

Our gate checks four things and would fail on any single one of them. A completed exchange proves reachability, matching MTUs prove the negotiation settled where we wanted, a pause rate within threshold proves the congestion handling behaves, and a stable carrier proves the link is not flapping. Each check reuses code from earlier in this chapter, which is why the gate itself is fifteen lines rather than a hundred.

We will now draw the decision our gate makes:

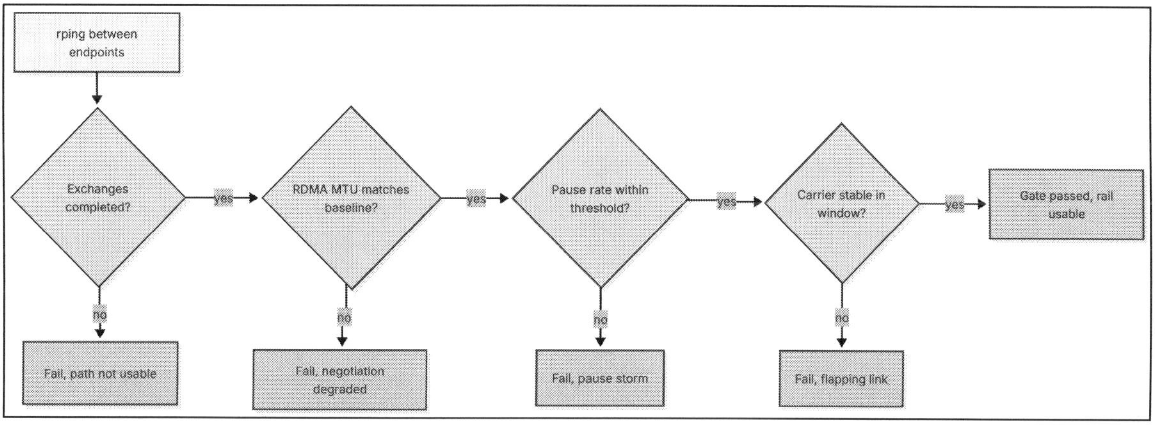

Single Report Cluster Team

A fabric report differs from a compliance report in one respect, since its audience thinks in rails and jobs rather than in ports. Our report therefore groups every finding by rail, names the accelerators affected, and states what a job crossing that rail would experience. Somebody deciding whether to drain a node needs that framing far more than a list of interface names.

We can now produce the report across live hosts and supplied fabric data together:

```
./build/debug/netops fabric report \
    --baseline lab/roce-fabric-baseline.yaml \
    --data data/fabric-rail3-captured.json \
    --live-hosts lab/gpu-nodes.csv \
    --out reports/fabric-2026-08-17.json
```

Here, all four rails report, and only one recommendation appears at the end.

```
netops: fabric report written to reports/fabric-2026-08-17.json
netops: baseline roce-fabric-baseline v4, 32 ports, 4 rails
netops: rail 0  healthy        8 accelerators
netops: rail 1  degraded       8 accelerators, pause storm on leaf-
04
netops: rail 2  degraded       8 accelerators, flapping link on
leaf-09
netops: rail 3  non-lossless   8 accelerators, pfc absent on leaf-
07 Ethernet12
netops: recommendation, drain rail 2 before the next scheduled run
```

That final recommendation is the only place in this book where our tool advises rather than reports. Our reasoning stays visible, since a flapping link degrades every job crossing it while a missing flow control configuration degrades only the jobs which saturate a link. We recommend and never act, exactly as we refused to remove a package from a production database in an earlier chapter. A cluster team owns the drain decision, and a fabric which degrades quietly needs a tool which speaks up on their behalf.

Summary

We have now automated the fabric which carries collective traffic, without ever writing verbs code. Our SoftRoCE setup gave every exercise a real device on an ordinary host, and our discovery reads device and port attributes identically against rxe and against four hundred gigabit hardware. The RDMA MTU turned out to be the value worth asserting rather than the interface MTU, since negotiation falls to 1024 bytes whenever the underlay disappoints it.

Our lossless baseline named priority, flow control, congestion thresholds, and trust mode as facts, and the validator found one non-lossless port among thirty-two in the supplied fabric data. The link statistics, read as rates rather than as totals, then revealed a pause storm and a flapping port which every status check had reported as healthy. A topology parser caught a collective falling back from RDMA, and our gate proved the path with rping before any workload arrived. In the next chapter, we put this fabric under a serving workload.

Chapter 11
Serving LLM, vLLM, and MCP Networking

Our fabric now carries collective traffic and proves that it does. A serving workload places quite different demands on the same hardware, because inference traffic arrives from outside, varies by the second, and must respond inside a budget somebody perceives. Nothing about a training run prepares us for that. This chapter builds the network path around a model server, from the gateway which admits a request to the replica which produces tokens.

We will now deploy a vLLM replica set at a pinned version on a processor-only path, read replica state rather than guessing at it, and tune the streaming transport where token latency actually goes. A router written in C++ then chooses replicas by load rather than in turn, holds session affinity without a sticky cookie, and scales the replica set on queue depth. An MCP server closes the chapter.

What Inference Traffic Actually Looks Like

Two Phases, Two Very Different Profiles

A single request passes through two phases with almost nothing in common. The first phase reads the whole prompt at once and builds the model state for it, which saturates compute and finishes in one burst. The second phase then produces one token at a time, each depending on the one before, which barely touches compute and instead waits on memory. Our network sees a small request followed by a long thin stream of tiny responses.

Such asymmetry decides how we route and how we tune. A replica busy in the first phase cannot serve new work usefully, while a replica producing tokens has capacity to spare. Any round-robin distribution therefore performs badly, since it ignores which phase each replica currently occupies. We keep the mechanics of the internal state transfer well outside our scope, and we care intensely about the load signal it produces. One consequence shapes the whole chapter, because every token travels as its own small message, so per-message overhead dominates rather than bandwidth. A stream producing forty tokens each second sends forty framed messages each second, every one carrying perhaps four bytes of payload. The Nagle algorithm, the keepalive intervals, and the flow control windows therefore matter far more here than the link rate we celebrated in the previous chapter.

Latency Somebody Notices

Two numbers describe the experience, and confusing them wastes a lot of tuning effort. The time to first token measures how long somebody stares at nothing, and queueing plus the first phase dominate it. Its companion, the time for each output token, measures how quickly the reply then unfolds, and the second phase plus our transport dominate that. A fast overall completion with a slow first token still feels broken to a person.

Our instrumentation therefore records both separately for every request. We stamp arrival, first byte of the first token, and completion, then report percentiles across a window rather than averages. An average hides the tail entirely, and the tail is what generates complaints. Our earlier habit of reading rates rather than totals applies here in a slightly different form.

We can now place the request path in front of us:

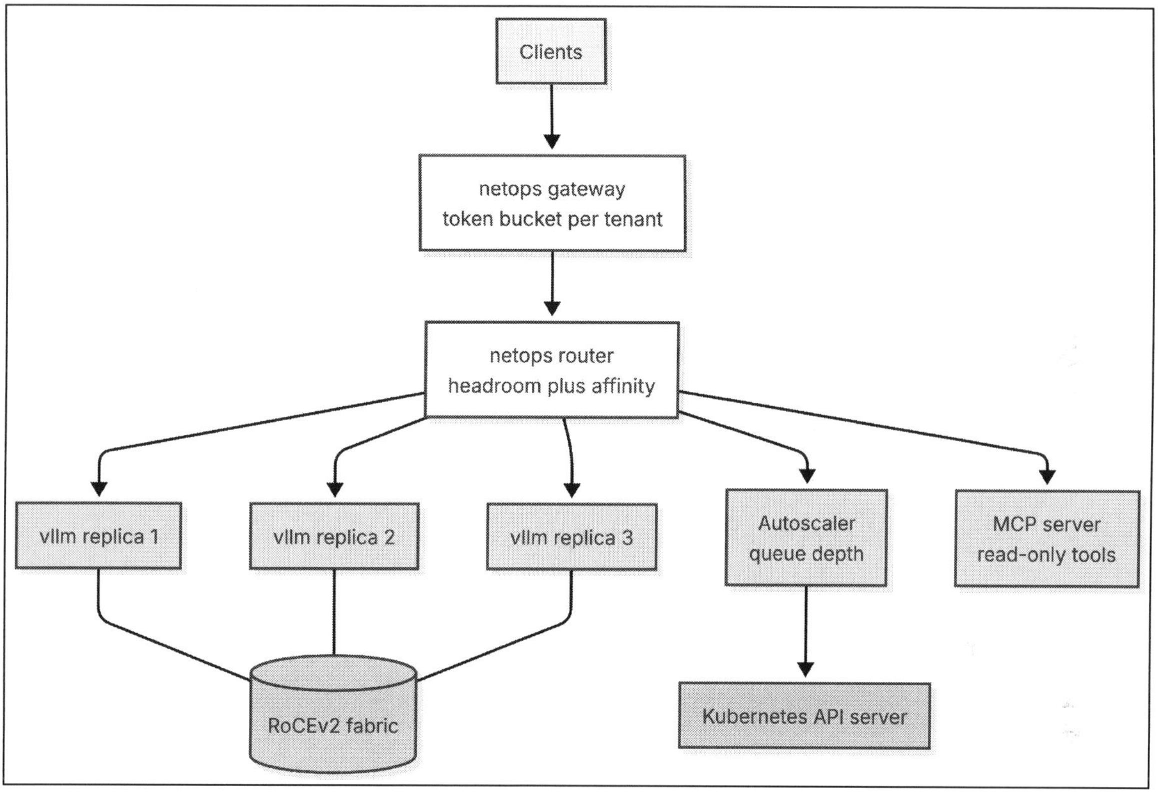

Standing up vLLM Replica Set

Pinned Version and Small Model

Every serving stack moves quickly, and a listing which worked six months ago frequently does not. We therefore pin an exact vLLM version in the manifest and in the repository, and we name a model small enough to load without an accelerator. A sub-billion parameter model produces tokens slowly on a processor and produces them correctly, which is all our routing and transport work actually requires.

In the following script, we will declare a three-replica deployment with bounded concurrency:

```
apiVersion: apps/v1
kind: Deployment
metadata:
  name: vllm-small
  namespace: blue
```

```yaml
  labels:
    netops.io/segment: inference
spec:
  replicas: 3
  selector:
    matchLabels: { app: vllm-small }
  template:
    metadata:
      labels: { app: vllm-small }
    spec:
      containers:
        - name: server
          image: vllm/vllm-openai:v0.9.2
          args:
            - --model=Qwen/Qwen2.5-0.5B-Instruct
            - --device=cpu
            - --max-model-len=2048
            - --max-num-seqs=8
            - --port=8000
          ports:
            - containerPort: 8000
              name: http
          readinessProbe:
            httpGet: { path: /health, port: 8000 }
            initialDelaySeconds: 40
            periodSeconds: 5
```

That **`max-num-seqs`** value of eight is our concurrency limit for each replica, and it becomes the denominator in every load calculation which follows. A replica admitting unlimited sequences appears healthy while its per-token latency collapses, so we bound it deliberately. Our readiness probe also waits forty seconds before its first attempt, because a model load reports failure otherwise and the whole deployment thrashes.

Reading Replica State

A router which guesses at replica load routes badly, and vLLM removes any need to guess. The server publishes metrics naming running sequences, waiting sequences, and cache utilisation, which together describe exactly the state our routing depends upon. We scrape those figures on a short interval and keep them beside each replica record. Nothing about the scrape is clever, and skipping it is what makes most routers useless.

Let us now read the three figures which drive every later decision:

```cpp
Result<ReplicaState> scrape_replica(EndpointClient& http, const
Replica& r) {
```

```
    auto body = http.get(r.address, 8000, "/metrics");
    if (!body) {
        return std::unexpected(body.error());
    }

    ReplicaState s{.address = r.address, .at =
std::chrono::steady_clock::now()};
    for (std::string_view line : lines_of(*body)) {
        if (line.starts_with('#')) {
            continue;
        }
        if (line.starts_with("vllm:num_requests_running")) {
            s.running = last_field_as_double(line);
        } else if (line.starts_with("vllm:num_requests_waiting")) {
            s.waiting = last_field_as_double(line);
        } else if (line.starts_with("vllm:gpu_cache_usage_perc")) {
            s.cache_used = last_field_as_double(line);
        }
    }

    s.headroom = std::max(0.0, r.max_seqs - s.running - s.waiting);
    return s;
}
```

In the following scrape, three replicas report, and their headroom figures differ far more than their health does.

```
netops: scraping 3 vllm replicas on inference segment
  replica               running  waiting  cache  headroom
  10.244.1.14:8000            6        2   0.71       0.0
  10.244.2.9:8000             3        0   0.38       5.0
  10.244.3.7:8000             1        0   0.12       7.0
netops: capacity 24 sequences, 12 in flight, 12 free, elapsed 0.03
s
```

Our first replica reports zero headroom while remaining perfectly healthy, which is precisely the situation round-robin cannot see. Two of its sequences already wait rather than run, so another request there would queue behind them. The third replica meanwhile sits nearly idle with a cold cache. Any routing decision made without those three rows is a guess dressed up as an algorithm.

Tuning Streaming Transport

A stream of tiny messages meets several mechanisms designed for bulk transfer, and each one adds delay. One of them, the Nagle algorithm, holds a small write while waiting for more data to accumulate, which suits a file copy and ruins a token stream. The delayed acknowledgement on the receiving side then compounds the effect. Our first tuning step therefore disables Nagle on every streaming connection, and the improvement is usually visible immediately. Two further settings matter almost as much, since an HTTP/2 flow control window sized for bulk transfer wastes nothing here, whereas a window sized too small stalls a stream every few tokens. Our keepalive intervals then decide how quickly we notice a replica which stopped responding midway through a stream.

At this point, we will apply both sets of options, one for raw sockets and one for gRPC channels:

```
void tune_stream(boost::asio::ip::tcp::socket& sock) {
    boost::system::error_code ec;
    sock.set_option(boost::asio::ip::tcp::no_delay(true), ec);
    sock.set_option(boost::asio::socket_base::keep_alive(true),
ec);

    const int idle = 15, interval = 5, probes = 3;
    const int fd = sock.native_handle();
    ::setsockopt(fd, IPPROTO_TCP, TCP_KEEPIDLE, &idle,
sizeof(idle));
    ::setsockopt(fd, IPPROTO_TCP, TCP_KEEPINTVL, &interval,
sizeof(interval));
    ::setsockopt(fd, IPPROTO_TCP, TCP_KEEPCNT, &probes,
sizeof(probes));
}

grpc::ChannelArguments streaming_channel_args() {
    grpc::ChannelArguments args;
    args.SetInt(GRPC_ARG_KEEPALIVE_TIME_MS, 15'000);
    args.SetInt(GRPC_ARG_KEEPALIVE_TIMEOUT_MS, 5'000);
    args.SetInt(GRPC_ARG_KEEPALIVE_PERMIT_WITHOUT_CALLS, 1);
    args.SetInt(GRPC_ARG_HTTP2_MAX_PINGS_WITHOUT_DATA, 0);
    args.SetInt(GRPC_ARG_HTTP2_BDP_PROBE, 1);
    return args;
}
```

Below, two hundred requests through three configurations show where the delay was hiding.

```
netops: transport comparison, 200 requests, 128 tokens each
  setting                    ttft p50   ttft p99   tpot p50   tpot
p99
```

```
  defaults                     412 ms     1840 ms      48 ms
186 ms
  no_delay only                402 ms     1795 ms      26 ms
94 ms
  no_delay plus keepalive      399 ms     1102 ms      26 ms
61 ms
netops: tpot p99 reduced 67 percent, ttft p99 reduced 40 percent
```

We halved our median per-token latency by disabling Nagle, and keepalives then cut the tail almost in half again. Neither change touched the model, the hardware, or the fabric. That second improvement deserves an explanation, since a keepalive makes nothing inherently faster. What it does is detect a dead connection within twenty seconds rather than within two minutes, which removes the worst outliers from the distribution entirely.

Cache-Aware Router

Least Loaded

Our router now holds three rows of truth for every replica, so the selection becomes arithmetic rather than rotation. We score each replica on available headroom, discount those carrying waiting sequences, and prefer a warm cache whenever headroom ties. Any replica reporting no headroom drops out of consideration entirely. Such a rule keeps a saturated replica from accepting work which would simply queue behind eight others.

In the following script, we will score every replica and shed when none can serve:

```
Result<Replica> Router::choose(const RequestContext& ctx) {
    auto snapshot = states_.load();
    if (snapshot->empty()) {
        return fail(Category::validation, ENOENT, "no replicas
known");
    }

    const Replica* best = nullptr;
    double best_score = -1.0;

    for (const ReplicaState& s : *snapshot) {
        if (s.headroom <= 0.0 || s.stale(std::chrono::seconds(5)))
{
            continue;
        }
        const double score = s.headroom
                           - 0.5 * s.waiting
                           + (ctx.warm_on(s.address) ? 2.0 : 0.0);
```

```
        if (score > best_score) {
            best_score = score;
            best = s.replica;
        }
    }

    if (best == nullptr) {
        return fail(Category::timeout, EBUSY,
                    "every replica saturated, request shed");
    }
    return *best;
}
```

That staleness check protects us from the worst available failure. A replica whose metrics stopped arriving five seconds ago may be dead, overloaded, or partitioned, and routing to it on the strength of stale figures sends work into a hole. We treat silence as unavailability rather than as continuity. Our shed path then returns a clear rejection instead of a timeout, which lets a client retry somewhere useful.

Session Affinity without Sticky Cookie

A conversation continuing across several requests benefits enormously from reaching the same replica, since the earlier state already sits resident there. A sticky cookie achieves that and then breaks whenever a replica leaves. We instead hash the session identifier across the live replica set with consistent hashing, so a departing replica redistributes only its own share rather than reshuffling everybody.

So here, we will then build the ring and look up a preferred replica:

```
class AffinityRing {
public:
    void rebuild(std::span<const Replica> live, unsigned vnodes =
128) {
        ring_.clear();
        for (const Replica& r : live) {
            for (unsigned v = 0; v < vnodes; ++v) {
                const auto key = std::hash<std::string>{}(
                    std::format("{}#{}", r.address, v));
                ring_.insert_or_assign(key, &r);
            }
        }
    }

    const Replica* preferred(std::string_view session) const {
        if (ring_.empty()) {
```

```
            return nullptr;
        }
        const auto h = std::hash<std::string_view>{}(session);
        auto it = ring_.lower_bound(h);
        if (it == ring_.end()) {
            it = ring_.begin();
        }
        return it->second;
    }

private:
    std::flat_map<std::size_t, const Replica*> ring_;
};
```

Our affinity remains a preference rather than a rule, and that distinction is what keeps us safe. The router consults the ring first, checks whether the preferred replica still holds headroom, and falls back to the least loaded choice when it does not. A strict affinity would queue a conversation behind a saturated replica purely for cache warmth, which trades a large latency cost against a small one. We take the warm path only when it happens also to be the free path.

Scaling and Admission

Autoscaling on Queue Depth

The processor utilisation figure is the wrong signal for scaling a model server, since the second phase barely uses the processor while people wait. The right signal is queue depth, because a waiting sequence is somebody staring at nothing. Our autoscaler therefore reads waiting sequences across the replica set and adjusts the replica figure through the API server we already speak to.

We can now reconcile the replica figure against measured pressure:

```
Result<void> Autoscaler::reconcile(std::span<const ReplicaState>
states) {
    double waiting = 0.0, capacity = 0.0;
    for (const ReplicaState& s : states) {
        waiting += s.waiting;
        capacity += s.headroom + s.running;
    }

    const double pressure = capacity > 0.0 ? waiting / capacity :
1.0;
    const int current = static_cast<int>(states.size());
    int wanted = current;
```

```
    if (pressure > 0.30 && current < max_replicas_) {
        wanted = std::min(max_replicas_, current + std::max(1,
current / 2));
    } else if (pressure < 0.02 && current > min_replicas_) {
        wanted = current - 1;
    }

    if (wanted == current) {
        return {};
    }
    if (clock_.now() - last_change_ < cooldown_) {
        return {};
    }

    last_change_ = clock_.now();
    return
kube_.apply("/apis/apps/v1/namespaces/blue/deployments/vllm-small",
                        replica_patch(wanted));
}
```

Our scale-up adds half the current replica set while scale-down removes one at a time, and the asymmetry is entirely deliberate. A queue building quickly needs relief now, whereas a quiet period may end at any moment and a model load costs forty seconds. The cooldown then prevents oscillation, since a replica scaled away disappears from the metrics only once it has fully gone. Both details come from watching autoscalers misbehave rather than from theory.

Rate Limiting at Gateway

A model server saturated by one caller serves nobody well, and admission control is far cheaper than any amount of scaling. Our gateway holds a token bucket for each tenant, refills it at an agreed rate, and rejects overflow with a clear status and a retry hint. An early rejection costs one lock acquisition, whereas admitting work we cannot serve costs a replica slot and somebody's patience.

In the following script, we will implement the bucket together with its retry hint:

```
class TokenBucket {
public:
    TokenBucket(double per_second, double burst)
        : rate_(per_second), burst_(burst), available_(burst) {}

    bool try_admit(double cost = 1.0) {
        const auto now = std::chrono::steady_clock::now();
        const double elapsed =
            std::chrono::duration<double>(now - refilled_).count();
```

```
        available_ = std::min(burst_, available_ + elapsed *
rate_);
        refilled_ = now;

        if (available_ < cost) {
            return false;
        }
        available_ -= cost;
        return true;
    }

    std::chrono::milliseconds retry_after(double cost = 1.0) const
{
        const double deficit = std::max(0.0, cost - available_);
        return std::chrono::milliseconds(
            static_cast<long>(1000.0 * deficit / rate_));
    }

private:
    double rate_, burst_, available_;
    std::chrono::steady_clock::time_point refilled_ =
        std::chrono::steady_clock::now();
};
```

One refinement makes the bucket fair rather than merely protective. A request asking for two thousand tokens costs far more than one asking for fifty, so we charge the bucket by requested length instead of by request. Our cost function uses the maximum token figure the caller declared, and we reject any caller who declines to declare one. Such weighting stops a single large request from consuming a replica while ten small ones wait.

MCP Server in C++

JSON-RPC over 'stdio' and HTTP

The Model Context Protocol carries a simple idea, namely that a model client can discover and call tools which somebody else implemented. No official C++ implementation exists, and the protocol is plain JSON-RPC over either standard streams or HTTP. Both transports suit us perfectly, and building the server ourselves teaches the protocol rather than a wrapper. We pin the specification revision in our repository, because the protocol still moves between releases.

Our next step is to implement the three methods a useful server must handle:

```
Result<void> McpServer::serve_stdio() {
    std::string line;
```

```
    while (std::getline(std::cin, line)) {
        const auto req = nlohmann::json::parse(line, nullptr,
false);
        if (req.is_discarded()) {
            reply(error_object(nullptr, -32700, "parse error"));
            continue;
        }

        const auto method = req.value("method", "");
        const auto id = req.contains("id") ? req["id"] :
nlohmann::json();

        if (method == "initialize") {
            reply(result_object(id, {
                {"protocolVersion", protocol_version_},
                {"serverInfo", {{"name", "netops"}, {"version",
"0.1.0"}}},
                {"capabilities", {{"tools",
nlohmann::json::object()}}}}));
        } else if (method == "tools/list") {
            reply(result_object(id, {{"tools",
registry_.describe()}}));
        } else if (method == "tools/call") {
            auto out = registry_.invoke(
                req["params"].value("name", ""),
                req["params"].value("arguments",
nlohmann::json::object()));
            if (!out) {
                reply(error_object(id, -32000,
out.error().detail));
            } else {
                reply(result_object(id, {{"content", *out}}));
            }
        } else if (!id.is_null()) {
            reply(error_object(id, -32601, "method not found"));
        }
    }
    return {};
}
```

That null identifier branch separates a working server from a puzzling one. A JSON-RPC notification carries no identifier and must receive no reply, so replying to one confuses every well-behaved client. Our handler therefore checks for an identifier before emitting any error at all. We reply to a parse failure with a null identifier, since the specification asks for precisely that.

We will now trace one client session through the protocol:

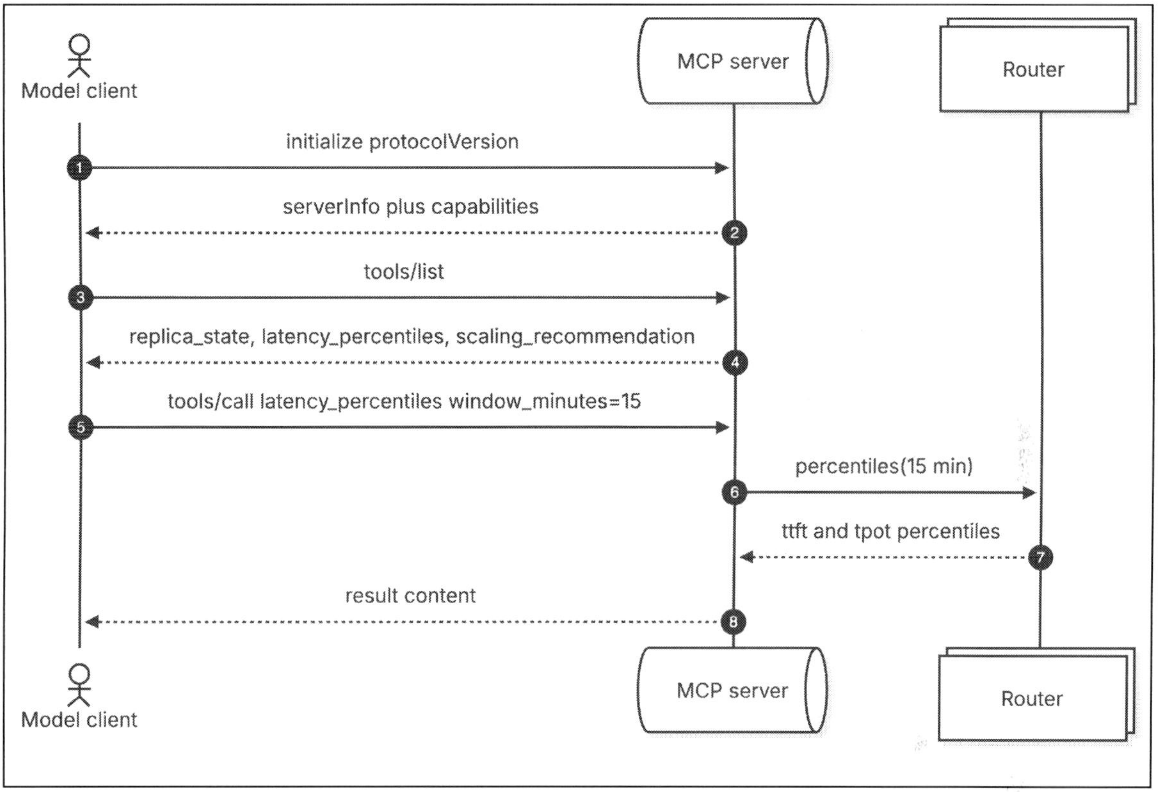

Exposing Router as Tools

Our router already holds facts somebody would want to ask about, and a tool is simply a named function carrying a described schema. We expose three, namely a replica state listing, a latency percentile query, and a scaling recommendation. Every one of them reads and none of them writes, which is a deliberate boundary rather than a limitation.

From here, we will register those three tools with their schemas and their validation:

```
void register_router_tools(ToolRegistry& reg, Router& router) {
    reg.add({.name = "replica_state",
             .description = "Current load and headroom for every
replica",
             .schema = nlohmann::json{{"type", "object"},
                                       {"properties",
nlohmann::json::object()}}},
            [&router](const nlohmann::json&) ->
Result<nlohmann::json> {
                return router.snapshot_as_json();
            });
```

```
    reg.add({.name = "latency_percentiles",
             .description = "First token and per-token latency
percentiles",
             .schema = nlohmann::json{
                 {"type", "object"},
                 {"properties", {{"window_minutes",
                                  {{"type", "integer"}, {"minimum",
1}}}}}},
                 {"required",
nlohmann::json::array({"window_minutes"})}}},
            [&router](const nlohmann::json& args) ->
Result<nlohmann::json> {
                const int m = args.value("window_minutes", 5);
                if (m < 1 || m > 1440) {
                    return fail(Category::validation, EINVAL,
                                "window_minutes must fall between 1
and 1440");
                }
                return router.percentiles(std::chrono::minutes(m));
            });

    reg.add({.name = "scaling_recommendation",
             .description = "Replica figure the autoscaler would
request now",
             .schema = nlohmann::json{{"type", "object"},
                                      {"properties",
nlohmann::json::object()}}},
            [&router](const nlohmann::json&) ->
Result<nlohmann::json> {
                return router.scaling_recommendation();
            });
}
```

We can now run the gateway, the router, the autoscaler, and the MCP server together:

```
./build/debug/netops serve \
    --replicas-selector app=vllm-small --namespace blue \
    --listen 0.0.0.0:9000 --mcp-stdio \
    --tenant-rate acme=20/s --tenant-rate beta=5/s
```

Every component reports, and the latency figures match the tuned configuration.

```
netops: 3 replicas discovered, capacity 24 sequences
netops: mcp server ready, protocolVersion 2025-06-18, 3 tools
registered
netops: gateway listening on 0.0.0.0:9000, 2 tenants configured
```

```
netops: routed 4180 requests, 0 shed, 12 affinity hits, 3 affinity
fallbacks
netops: ttft p50 399 ms, p99 1102 ms
netops: tpot p50 26 ms, p99 61 ms
netops: autoscaler raised replicas 3 -> 4 at pressure 0.34
netops: tenant beta rejected 61 requests, retry-after 200 ms median
```

Those three affinity fallbacks against twelve hits make a healthy ratio rather than a fault. Each fallback means a conversation reached a different replica because its preferred one held no headroom, which is exactly the trade we chose deliberately. Our rejected requests belong to the tenant whose agreed rate was five each second, and the retry hint tells their client when to return. Everything in that summary came from figures we scraped rather than from assumptions, which is the whole point, because a router only routes well when it knows something true about every destination.

Summary

We have now built the network path around a model server rather than around a training job. Two phases with opposite profiles explained why round-robin distribution performs badly, and three scraped figures for every replica replaced the guessing which usually stands in for load. The transport tuning then halved our median per-token latency and cut the tail by two thirds, without touching the model, the hardware, or the fabric.

Our router scores replicas on headroom, treats stale metrics as unavailability, and holds session affinity as a preference rather than a rule. The autoscaler reads queue depth instead of processor utilisation, scales up faster than it scales down, and respects a cooldown. A token bucket charged by requested length keeps one caller from starving the rest, and an MCP server built directly on JSON-RPC exposes three read-only tools.

CHAPTER 12
TELEMETRY, OBSERVABILITY, AND AI-ASSISTED OPERATIONS

The eleven chapters behind us have given our tool the ability to change things and to prove those changes worked. This final chapter turns that ability inward, so the tool watches continuously rather than only during a rollout. The telemetry arrives from switches, from accelerators, and from the router we built last, and somebody has to decide which of it matters. We build that decision here, and we build the restraint which must accompany it.

We will now stream telemetry through a pipeline which respects cardinality, export it through OpenTelemetry, and detect trouble with thresholds, rolling statistics, and a pre-trained model for the awkward cases. A capacity forecast then warns us before a wall arrives, and a closed loop drains a failing node and requeues its work. Our MCP registry grows to carry telemetry, which lets a model assist with triage.

Collecting Telemetry

Streaming Subscriptions

Our gNMI client from an earlier chapter already streams state, so nothing new is needed at the transport layer. What we need now is a decision about what to subscribe to, and that decision determines whether our pipeline survives a large fabric. A subscription asking for every leaf under every interface produces millions of updates each second and teaches us nothing at all. We therefore declare a subscription plan as data and review it like any other configuration.

In the following script, we will declare the paths, the modes, and the exclusions:

```
name: fabric-telemetry
version: 3

subscriptions:
  - path: /interfaces/interface/state/oper-status
    mode: on_change
  - path: /interfaces/interface/state/counters/in-errors
    mode: sample
    interval: 30s
  - path:
/qos/interfaces/interface/output/queues/queue/state/dropped-pkts
    mode: sample
    interval: 30s
  - path: /components/component/state/temperature/instant
    mode: sample
    interval: 60s

drop:
  - path_suffix: /state/counters/in-octets
    reason: "carried by the fabric report, not needed every second"
```

Here, two modes appear, and choosing between them is most of the skill. An on-change subscription suits anything which stays still for hours and matters immediately, such as an operational state. A sample subscription suits anything which moves continuously, since on-change against such a leaf floods us with noise. Our plan also carries an explicit drop list, which earned its place after exactly one incident. A firmware upgrade introduced per-queue statistics beneath a path we had wildcarded, and our ingest rate rose forty-fold overnight. An explicit deny list gives us somewhere to record the decision alongside its reasoning, so anybody reviewing the plan a year later reads why a leaf is excluded rather than guessing at it.

Cardinality and Real Budget

Our storage costs scale with the number of distinct series rather than with the volume of samples, and that distinction surprises people repeatedly. A metric carrying labels for the interface, the switch, and the queue produces a manageable family. The same metric with a label for the flow identifier produces a fresh series for every conversation, which exhausts any backend within days. Our pipeline therefore enforces an allowlist of labels rather than passing through whatever happens to arrive.

Let us now admit series against both an allowlist and a budget:

```
class CardinalityGuard {
public:
    CardinalityGuard(std::vector<std::string> allowed, std::size_t
budget)
        : allowed_(std::move(allowed)), budget_(budget) {}

    Result<Series> admit(Series s) {
        std::erase_if(s.labels, [this](const auto& kv) {
            return !std::ranges::contains(allowed_, kv.first);
        });

        const auto key = s.fingerprint();
        if (!seen_.contains(key) && seen_.size() >= budget_) {
            ++rejected_;
            return fail(Category::validation, ENOSPC,
                        std::format("series budget {} exhausted,
dropped {}",
                                    budget_, s.name));
        }
        seen_.insert(key);
        return s;
    }

    std::size_t distinct() const { return seen_.size(); }
    std::size_t rejected() const { return rejected_; }
```

```
private:
    std::vector<std::string> allowed_;
    std::size_t budget_;
    std::flat_set<std::size_t> seen_;
    std::size_t rejected_ = 0;
};
```

Our guard rejects rather than truncates once the budget is reached, and it reports how often that happens. A pipeline which silently discards the newest series hides a configuration mistake for months, whereas a rejection figure on a dashboard invites the obvious question. We set the budget deliberately low at first and raise it after review. Such a habit turns cardinality from an incident into a conversation.

From here, we will picture the whole pipeline before we build the rest of it:

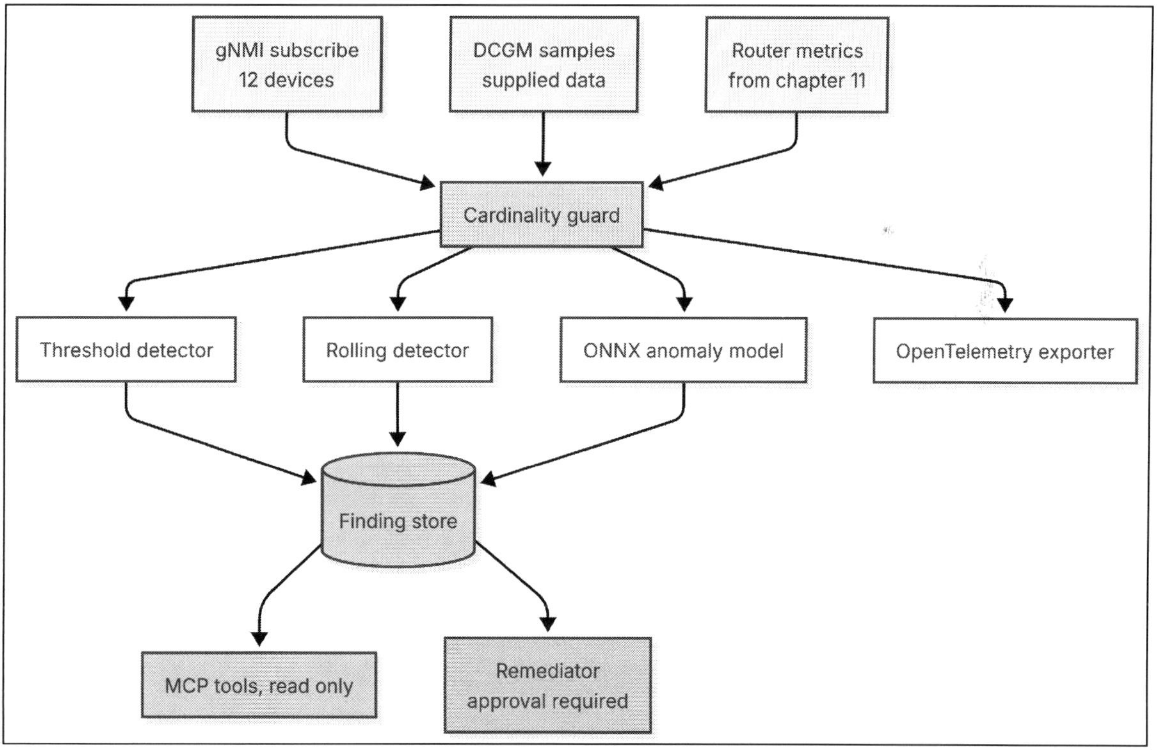

Exporting through OpenTelemetry

Single Pipeline for Multiple Destinations

Every organisation eventually wants telemetry in two places at once, typically a metrics backend and a longer-term store. We would rather not write an exporter for each one, since that is work nobody enjoys doing twice. The OpenTelemetry libraries give us one instrumentation surface and move the destination question into configuration, which is exactly the separation we have used for transports throughout this book. Our collectors record into instruments and never learn where the data lands.

We will now initialise the exporter, the reader, and the resource together:

```
Result<void> init_telemetry(const TelemetryConfig& cfg) {
    otlp::OtlpGrpcMetricExporterOptions opts;
    opts.endpoint = cfg.otlp_endpoint;
    opts.use_ssl_credentials = cfg.tls;

    auto exporter =
otlp::OtlpGrpcMetricExporterFactory::Create(opts);
    if (!exporter) {
        return fail(Category::internal, EIO, "otlp exporter not
created");
    }

    metric_sdk::PeriodicExportingMetricReaderOptions reader_opts;
    reader_opts.export_interval_millis =
std::chrono::milliseconds(cfg.interval);
    reader_opts.export_timeout_millis =
std::chrono::milliseconds(5000);

    auto reader =
metric_sdk::PeriodicExportingMetricReaderFactory::Create(
        std::move(exporter), reader_opts);

    auto resource = sdk::resource::Resource::Create({
        {"service.name", "netops"},
        {"service.version", cfg.version},
        {"deployment.environment", cfg.environment},
        {"netops.fabric", cfg.fabric_name},
        {"netops.rail", cfg.rail}});

    auto provider = metric_sdk::MeterProviderFactory::Create(
        std::make_unique<metric_sdk::ViewRegistry>(), resource);
    static_cast<metric_sdk::MeterProvider*>(provider.get())
        ->AddMetricReader(std::move(reader));

    metrics_api::Provider::SetMeterProvider(std::move(provider));
    return {};
}
```

That export timeout of five seconds against an interval of ten is a ratio worth keeping. A timeout longer than the interval lets exports overlap and queue, which turns a slow backend into a memory problem inside our own process. We would far rather drop one export window and record the failure. Our earlier spool discipline from the detection chapter applies whenever the data genuinely must not be lost.

Resource Attributes for Queries

The resource attributes decide whether anybody can query our telemetry usefully in six months. A metric tagged only with a hostname forces every enquiry to begin from a name somebody must already know. The same metric tagged with the fabric and the rail lets a query ask about a rail directly, which is how a cluster team actually thinks about a failure. Our previous work on fabric health made that grouping essential rather than merely convenient.

One rule keeps attributes useful over time. An attribute must describe where the measurement came from rather than what it means, since meaning belongs in the metric name. A rail number, a fabric name, and an environment all describe origin, whereas a severity or a threshold does not. We reject any attribute which changes for the same source, because such a label multiplies series without adding information.

Earned Alerts

Thresholds and Rolling Statistics

A threshold is the right tool whenever we know the limit, and a considerable number of limits are genuinely known. An interface which is down is down, a temperature above the specified maximum is a fault, and a pause rate of eighteen thousand each second is a storm. Nothing about those needs statistics. Our detector therefore checks the known limits first, because a threshold breach costs almost nothing to compute and is easy to explain afterwards. A rolling statistic then handles everything else, since a drop rate of forty each second means nothing without knowing that this port normally drops two, and no fixed threshold serves every port across a fabric. We maintain an exponentially weighted mean and variance for each series, then flag any value which departs from its own history. Such a detector learns the normal behaviour of each port without anybody configuring a single number.

Now we will implement the rolling detector with a warm-up period:

```
class RollingDetector {
public:
    RollingDetector(double alpha, double z_threshold, unsigned
warmup)
        : alpha_(alpha), z_(z_threshold), warmup_(warmup) {}

    std::optional<Finding> observe(const Series& s, double value) {
        auto& st = state_[s.fingerprint()];
```

```
        ++st.samples;

        if (st.samples <= warmup_) {
            st.mean = st.samples == 1 ? value
                                      : st.mean + alpha_ * (value -
st.mean);
            st.var = std::max(1e-9, st.var + alpha_ *
                                  ((value - st.mean) * (value -
st.mean) - st.var));
            return std::nullopt;
        }

        const double sigma = std::sqrt(st.var);
        const double score = std::abs(value - st.mean) / sigma;

        st.mean += alpha_ * (value - st.mean);
        st.var += alpha_ * ((value - st.mean) * (value - st.mean) -
st.var);

        if (score < z_) {
            return std::nullopt;
        }
        return Finding{.host = s.label("switch"),
                       .fact = s.name,
                       .wanted = std::format("within {:.1f} sigma
of {:.2f}",
                                             z_, st.mean),
                       .observed = std::format("{:.2f} at {:.1f}
sigma",
                                               value, score),
                       .severity = score > 2 * z_ ? Severity::high
                                                  :
Severity::medium};
    }

private:
    struct St { double mean = 0.0, var = 1.0; unsigned samples = 0;
};
    double alpha_, z_;
    unsigned warmup_;
    std::flat_map<std::size_t, St> state_;
};
```

Across four thousand series, four findings surface, and two of them came from each detector.

```
netops: detection sweep, 18 min window, 4120 series
```

```
  kind      series                                    wanted
observed
  threshold  oper-status leaf-09 Ethernet4            UP
DOWN
  threshold  temperature spine-02 sensor-1            < 75 C
81 C
  rolling    dropped-pkts leaf-04 Eth7 queue-3        within 3.0
sigma  at 9.4 sigma
  rolling    in-errors leaf-11 Ethernet2              within 3.0
sigma  at 3.6 sigma
netops: 2 threshold findings, 2 rolling findings, 4116 series quiet
netops: warmup incomplete for 41 series, suppressed
```

That suppression line matters rather more than it looks. A detector alerting during its own warm-up produces a burst of noise every time we restart, which teaches everybody to ignore the whole system. We suppress until each series holds enough history to be judged, and we report how many remain suppressed. Anybody seeing forty-one suppressed series after an hour knows something restarted rather than assuming quiet.

Pre-Trained Model for Exceptions

There are faults which reveal themselves only in the relationship between several signals. A rising pause rate alone means congestion, whereas a rising pause rate with a falling completion rate and a stable error rate means something rather different. A rolling statistic applied to each series separately cannot see that pattern at all. We therefore load a small pre-trained model and run inference over a feature vector, which amounts to roughly twenty lines of glue. Two boundaries keep this inside our means, because we train nothing at all, and our repository ships the model as a file rather than as a pipeline. We also treat the output as a score feeding the same **`Finding`** shape as everything else, rather than as a verdict. Such framing keeps the model honest, since a score which disagrees with the thresholds simply produces two findings for a person to weigh.

Our next step is to run inference and reject a malformed feature vector before it reaches the model:

```
Result<double> AnomalyModel::score(std::span<const float> features)
{
    if (features.size() != input_width_) {
        return fail(Category::validation, EINVAL,
                    std::format("model expects {} features,
received {}",
                                input_width_, features.size()));
    }

    const std::array<std::int64_t, 2> shape{
        1, static_cast<std::int64_t>(input_width_)};
```

```
    auto input = Ort::Value::CreateTensor<float>(
        memory_info_, const_cast<float*>(features.data()),
features.size(),
        shape.data(), shape.size());

    const char* in_names[] = {"features"};
    const char* out_names[] = {"score"};

    auto outputs = session_.Run(Ort::RunOptions{nullptr}, in_names,
                                &input, 1, out_names, 1);
    if (outputs.empty()) {
        return fail(Category::internal, EIO, "model produced no
output");
    }
    return
static_cast<double>(*outputs.front().GetTensorData<float>());
}
```

One rail scores high, and the contributing signals travel alongside the score.

```
netops: anomaly model rail3-congestion-v2.onnx, 7 features, 1.2 MB
  rail   score   contributing signals
  0       0.08   none above baseline
  1       0.91   pause_rate high, completion_rate falling, errors
stable
  2       0.14   pause_rate slightly above baseline
netops: 1 finding, rail 1 pattern resembles a receiver-side stall
netops: inference 0.31 ms per rail, 3 rails scored
```

Our model names which signals contributed rather than reporting a bare score, and that difference decides whether anybody trusts it. A score of nought point nine one with no reasoning attached invites an argument, whereas the same score alongside three named signals invites a look at the receiver. We derive those contributions from feature magnitudes rather than from anything sophisticated. An honest attribution beats a better model nobody acts upon.

GPU Health and Capacity Forecasting

Reading DCGM against Supplied Data

The health of an accelerator lives outside the network and reaches us through DCGM, which reports temperature, throttling reasons, memory errors, and link state for every device. A cluster team cares about those alongside fabric health, because a job fails identically whether a rail broke or a device throttled. Our repository supplies captured output from a real eight-device node, so the parser and the rules both get written without any hardware.

In the following script, we will evaluate device health against a baseline which tolerates some throttling:

```
std::vector<Finding> evaluate_gpu_health(std::span<const GpuSample>
samples,
                                         const GpuBaseline& base) {
    std::vector<Finding> out;
    for (const GpuSample& g : samples) {
        const auto untolerated = g.throttle_reasons &
~base.tolerated_reasons;
        if (untolerated != 0) {
            out.push_back({.host = g.node, .fact = "gpu_throttle",
                           .wanted = "no untolerated throttling",
                           .observed =
describe_throttle(untolerated),
                           .severity = Severity::high});
        }
        if (g.ecc_uncorrected > 0) {
            out.push_back({.host = g.node, .fact = "gpu_ecc",
                           .wanted = "0 uncorrected errors",
                           .observed = std::format("{} on device
{}",

g.ecc_uncorrected, g.index),
                           .severity = Severity::high});
        }
        if (g.nvlink_down > 0) {
            out.push_back({.host = g.node, .fact = "nvlink",
                           .wanted = "all links up",
                           .observed = std::format("{} links down",
                                                   g.nvlink_down),
                           .severity = Severity::high});
        }
    }
    return out;
}
```

That tolerated reasons mask deserves a word, since not every throttle is a fault. A device reducing its clock because a power cap was configured deliberately behaves entirely correctly, whereas the same reduction from a thermal limit signals a cooling problem. Our baseline names which reasons we accept, and anything outside that set becomes a finding. Without the mask, a well-configured cluster reports high severity every minute and everybody stops reading.

Forecasting before Wall Arrives

A capacity wall arrives with plenty of warning, and almost nobody reads it. Our forecaster fits a trend across a rolling window and reports how many days remain until a resource reaches its limit. Nothing sophisticated is required, since a linear fit across four weeks predicts a fabric or a cluster well enough to act upon. What matters is reporting the figure somewhere a person looks at least weekly.

We will now fit the trend and refuse the cases which cannot yield a date:

```
Result<Forecast> forecast_exhaustion(std::span<const Sample>
history,
                                      double limit) {
    if (history.size() < 14) {
        return fail(Category::validation, ENODATA,
                    "at least 14 samples required for a trend");
    }

    double sx = 0, sy = 0, sxx = 0, sxy = 0;
    const double n = static_cast<double>(history.size());
    for (std::size_t i = 0; i < history.size(); ++i) {
        const double x = static_cast<double>(i);
        const double y = history[i].value;
        sx += x; sy += y; sxx += x * x; sxy += x * y;
    }

    const double denom = n * sxx - sx * sx;
    if (std::abs(denom) < 1e-9) {
        return fail(Category::validation, EINVAL, "degenerate
trend");
    }

    const double slope = (n * sxy - sx * sy) / denom;
    const double intercept = (sy - slope * sx) / n;

    if (slope <= 0.0) {
        return Forecast{.slope_per_day = slope, .days_remaining = -
1};
    }
    return Forecast{.slope_per_day = slope,
                    .days_remaining =
                        static_cast<int>(((limit - intercept) /
slope) - n)};
}
```

One resource crosses inside a fortnight, and the recommendation names a date.

```
netops: capacity forecast, 28 day window, limits from baseline
```

```
  resource                          now     limit   slope/day   days
left
  rail 0 peak utilisation          61 %      85 %      0.41 %
58
  rail 1 peak utilisation          78 %      85 %      0.94 %
7
  gpu allocatable rdma devices       14        32      -0.30
n/a
  spine uplink peak                44 %      80 %      0.12 %
300
netops: 1 forecast inside 14 days, rail 1 reaches its limit in 7
days
netops: recommendation, add rail 1 capacity or rebalance before 24
August
```

That horizon of seven days is enough warning to order nothing and rebalance something, which is precisely why the figure earns its place. Our forecaster reports a negative slope as no result rather than as an infinite runway, since a declining resource carries no exhaustion date at all. We also require fourteen samples before fitting anything, because a trend drawn from three points describes noise. Both refusals produce a shorter report which somebody actually reads.

Closing Loop Safely

Drain, Requeue and Verify

A finding which nobody acts upon is a finding which eventually stops being read. We can safely automate a few remediations, and draining a node with a failed accelerator is the clearest example we have. Our loop cordons the node, evicts its job workloads, verifies the migration, and records everything it did. Every step reuses machinery from earlier chapters rather than inventing a new mechanism.

In the following script, we will implement that loop with approval as its first gate:

```
Result<void> Remediator::drain_and_requeue(const Finding& f,
                                           const Approval&
approval) {
    if (!approval.granted_for(f)) {
        return fail(Category::validation, EPERM,
                    std::format("drain of {} requires approval",
f.host));
    }

    auto cordoned = kube_.apply(
        std::format("/api/v1/nodes/{}", f.host),
```

```
        nlohmann::json{{"spec", {{"unschedulable", true}}}});
    if (!cordoned) {
        return std::unexpected(cordoned.error());
    }

    auto pods = kube_.pods_on_node(f.host);
    if (!pods) {
        return std::unexpected(pods.error());
    }
    for (const auto& pod : *pods) {
        if (pod.owned_by_job()) {
            if (auto e = kube_.evict(pod); !e) {
                return std::unexpected(e.error());
            }
        }
    }

    auto migrated = kube_.watch_until(
        std::format("/api/v1/pods?fieldSelector=spec.nodeName={}",
f.host),
        std::chrono::minutes(10),
        [](const nlohmann::json& o) { return o["items"].empty();
});
    if (!migrated) {
        return std::unexpected(migrated.error());
    }

    journal_.record(f, "cordoned and drained", approval.by);
    return {};
}
```

One failing node is drained, and the replacement placement gets proven before we finish.

```
netops: finding gpu_ecc on gpu-node-07, 3 uncorrected errors,
severity high
netops: remediation drain_and_requeue requires approval
netops: approval granted by p.dhandre at 02:14 UTC
netops: cordoned gpu-node-07
netops: evicted 2 job pods, 1 daemonset pod left in place
netops: node empty of job workloads after 3 m 12 s
netops: requeued training-job-4471, rank 6 rescheduled to gpu-node-
09
netops: fabric gate passed on gpu-node-09, rail 2 healthy
netops: journal entry 0x3f18 written
```

Our loop verifies the outcome rather than trusting the eviction call. A pod evicted from one node and left pending on none is a worse outcome than the fault we responded to, so we watch until the node is empty and the replacement is running. The fabric gate from an earlier chapter then proves the new placement can carry collective traffic. Nothing gets marked remediated on the strength of an API response.

Rejecting Automation

One list matters more than anything else in this chapter, namely the list of things our tool will not do on its own. We refuse to push configuration to a device without approval, we refuse to remove capacity when doing so would drop a fabric below its redundancy floor, and we refuse to act on a finding produced solely by the model. Each refusal comes from a plausible failure rather than from vague caution.

Our third refusal deserves the fullest defence. A model score is a correlation across signals we happened to choose, and a change made on that basis alone cannot be reviewed by anybody afterwards. We therefore require a threshold or a rolling finding to accompany any automated action, with the model serving to raise priority rather than to authorise. Such a rule keeps the reasoning behind every action legible to a person.

AI-Assisted Operations

Telemetry as MCP Tools

Our MCP server from the previous chapter already exposes router state, and telemetry fits the same registry very naturally. We add tools for a metric query, a findings listing, and a capacity forecast. Every one of them reads, and the registry rejects any attempt to add a writing tool without an explicit capability flag. A model client can therefore ask anything at all and change nothing whatsoever.

To make that concrete, we will register the three telemetry tools with their validation:

```
void register_telemetry_tools(ToolRegistry& reg,
                              MetricStore& metrics,
                              FindingStore& findings,
                              Forecaster& forecaster) {
    reg.add({.name = "query_metric",
             .description = "Percentiles for one metric across a
window",
             .schema = metric_query_schema()},
            [&metrics](const nlohmann::json& a) ->
Result<nlohmann::json> {
                const auto name = a.value("name", "");
                if (!metrics.known(name)) {
```

```
                    return fail(Category::validation, EINVAL,
                                std::format("unknown metric '{}'",
name));
                }
                return metrics.percentiles(name, window_of(a));
            });

    reg.add({.name = "open_findings",
             .description = "Findings not yet remediated, newest
first",
             .schema = severity_filter_schema()},
            [&findings](const nlohmann::json& a) ->
Result<nlohmann::json> {
                return findings.open(min_severity_of(a));
            });

    reg.add({.name = "capacity_forecast",
             .description = "Days remaining until a resource
reaches its limit",
             .schema = resource_schema()},
            [&forecaster](const nlohmann::json& a) ->
Result<nlohmann::json> {
                return forecaster.as_json(a.value("resource", ""));
            });
}
```

That unknown metric rejection exists for a specific reason. A model asked about a metric which does not exist will often invent a plausible name, and a tool returning empty results for anything unknown quietly encourages the habit. We reject with the name we received, which prompts a correction rather than a confident emptiness. Such small refusals make the whole arrangement considerably more useful.

Triage, Correlation and Written Narrative

Our findings correlate with one another, and that is where a model genuinely helps. Any three findings arriving within a minute may be one fault seen from three angles, and to recognise that pattern from a plain description of each one is exactly the sort of work a model does well. Our tools supply the facts, and the model supplies the connective reasoning. Nothing about the arrangement requires the model to be right, because a person reads the result before acting.

A model client connected over our stdio transport produces the following during an incident.

```
netops-mcp session, 02:14 UTC

tools/call open_findings {"min_severity":"high"}
```

```
  -> 3 findings
     gpu_ecc    gpu-node-07  3 uncorrected errors
     nvlink     gpu-node-07  2 links down
     rolling    leaf-04 Ethernet7 dropped-pkts at 9.4 sigma

tools/call query_metric {"name":"nccl_allreduce_duration_ms",
                         "window_minutes":30}
  -> p50 41 ms, p99 2180 ms, previous window p99 46 ms

Assistant narrative:
  All three findings trace back to gpu-node-07. The uncorrected
memory
  errors and the two down NVLink connections point at one device
rather
  than at the fabric. The drop rate on leaf-04 Ethernet7 belongs to
the
  rail this node occupies, so the fabric symptom sits downstream of
the
  device fault. Collective duration at the 99th percentile rose
from
  46 ms to 2180 ms across the same window, which is consistent with
one
  straggling rank. Suggested action, drain gpu-node-07 and requeue.
  This narrative is advisory and no action has been taken.
```

That final line is not decoration. Our server appends it to every narrative, because a written recommendation reads as an instruction unless it plainly says otherwise. The reasoning above happens to be correct, and the value lies in the three tool calls rather than in the prose. Anybody could have reached the same conclusion in ten minutes, and at two in the morning ten minutes is very much the point.

Guardrails

Read-Only by Default

Our registry treats a writing tool as an exception requiring a flag, a capability, and an audit entry. A read-only default is the only posture which survives a mistake, since the worst outcome of a bad read is a confusing report. We also expose no tool which can modify our own configuration, because a model able to widen its own permissions holds no meaningful permissions at all.

One further boundary applies to the transport. Our MCP server binds to a local socket or runs over standard streams, and it refuses a network listener without both explicit configuration and mutual TLS. A telemetry interface reachable across a datacenter is an information disclosure waiting to happen. We learned the same lesson about an admin interface several chapters ago, and the reasoning has not changed since.

Validation and Approval for Writes

Any configuration a model helps to produce passes through exactly the same validation as configuration we wrote ourselves. Our libyang check from an earlier chapter runs first, the device validation RPC runs second, and a person approves before the commit. All three gates on a generated change may appear excessive until we recall that the first two run in microseconds and reject most mistakes outright.

We will now implement the guarded path which every write travels through:

```
Result<void> guarded_apply(const ChangePlan& plan,
                           const SchemaContext& schema,
                           const Approval& approval,
                           Executor& exec,
                           Journal& journal) {
    if (plan.origin == Origin::model_assisted &&
!approval.granted_for(plan)) {
        return fail(Category::validation, EPERM,
                    "model-assisted plans require named approval");
    }

    if (auto valid = validate(schema, plan); !valid) {
        journal.record(plan, "rejected by schema", approval.by);
        return std::unexpected(valid.error());
    }

    auto applied = exec.apply(plan);
    if (!applied) {
        journal.record(plan, "rejected by device", approval.by);
        return std::unexpected(applied.error());
    }

    journal.record(plan, "applied", approval.by);
    return {};
}
```

We can now run the whole system as one process:

```
./build/debug/netops aiops \
    --subscriptions lab/fabric-telemetry.yaml \
    --gpu-data data/dcgm-node07-captured.json \
    --model models/rail3-congestion-v2.onnx \
```

```
    --otlp http://collector.internal:4317 \
    --mcp-stdio --approvals required
```

Every component reports its own posture, and the system reaches steady state in about a minute.

```
netops: 4 subscriptions active on 12 devices, 4120 series admitted,
0 rejected
netops: otlp exporter healthy, 10 s interval, 0 dropped windows
netops: detectors armed, thresholds 18, rolling 4120, model 1
netops: mcp server ready, 6 tools registered, all read-only
netops: approvals required, journal at var/netops/journal.log
netops: steady state after 62 s
```

Every line in that summary describes a decision we made deliberately rather than a default we accepted. Our series admission reports zero rejections, our exporter reports zero dropped windows, and our registry reports six read-only tools. A steady state reached in sixty-two seconds covers the whole system, from a switch subscription through to a model client, running inside one process. Nothing in it acts without a name attached to the action.

Summary

We have now closed the loop which the opening chapter began. Our telemetry streams through a pipeline which respects cardinality rather than discovering it painfully, exports through OpenTelemetry with attributes a cluster team can query, and meets three layers of detection where each layer earns its alerts differently. The forecasting turned a capacity wall into a date on a calendar, and a closed loop drained a failing node before proving the replacement could carry collective traffic.

Our MCP registry then grew to six read-only tools, which let a model correlate three findings into one narrative while every write stayed behind schema validation, device validation, and a named approval. All twelve chapters have carried **`netops`** from a single translation unit to a system spanning switches, servers, overlays, clouds, clusters, fabrics, and inference. The discipline never changed across any of them. We read before writing, we prove after changing, and we leave a person in charge of the consequence.

Index

L

M

N

O

P

R

S

T

V

X

Y

Z

Thank You

Made in the USA
Coppell, TX
05 November 2026

11299169R00116